CAMBRIDGE
Global English

for Cambridge Secondary 1
English as a Second Language

Workbook

9

Chris Barker and Libby Mitchell

CAMBRIDGE
UNIVERSITY PRESS

CAMBRIDGE
UNIVERSITY PRESS

University Printing House, Cambridge CB2 8BS, United Kingdom

One Liberty Plaza, 20th Floor, New York, NY 10006, USA

477 Williamstown Road, Port Melbourne, VIC 3207, Australia

314–321, 3rd Floor, Plot 3, Splendor Forum, Jasola District Centre, New Delhi – 110025, India

103 Penang Road, #05-06/07, Visioncrest Commercial, Singapore 238467

Cambridge University Press is part of the University of Cambridge.

It furthers the University's mission by disseminating knowledge in the pursuit of education, learning and research at the highest international levels of excellence.

www.cambridge.org
Information on this title: www.cambridge.org/9781107635203

First published 2016

20 19 18 17 16 15 14 13 12

Printed in Malaysia by Vivar Printing

A catalogue record for this publication is available from the British Library

ISBN 978-1-107-63520-3 Paperback

All questions, answers and annotations have been written by the author.
In examinations, the way marks are awarded may be different.

Contents

1 Family ties

Family life

1 Solve the crossword.

Across

3 Your mother and father. (7)

4 I've got one _____ . She's my mother's sister. (4)

6 The daughter of your brother or your sister. (5)

7 I'm already an aunt because my eldest brother is _____ and has a baby daughter. (7)

8 Tom is my stepfather's son, so he's my _____ . (11)

10 Sara is my stepfather's daughter, so she's my _____ . (10)

11 The plural of *child*. (8)

12 My sister has got a son, so he's my _____ . (6)

13 Fred is my uncle by marriage. He's my aunt's _____ . (7)

Down

1 The opposite of *oldest*. (8)

2 Your grandmother and grandfather. (12)

5 I've got two _____: my father's brother and my mother's brother. (6)

8 Brothers and sisters. (8)

9 I haven't got any brothers and sisters but I don't mind being an _____ child. (4)

2 Look at the family tree. Write sentences saying who the following people are in relation to Zara.

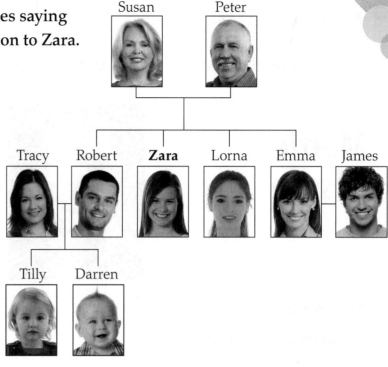

Susan   Peter

Tracy   Robert   **Zara**   Lorna   Emma   James

Tilly   Darren

1 Susan and Peter   *Susan and Peter are Zara's parents.*

2 Lorna and Emma   _____

3 Robert   _____

4 Tracy   _____

5 James   _____

6 Tilly and Darren   _____

3 **Read what Karen says about her family and answer the questions.**

1 Who is the eldest child in the family and who is the youngest? _____
_____

2 Who does Karen get on well with? _____

3 Who never gets told off? _____

4 Who gets away with doing nothing at home?
_____

5 Why is Karen annoyed? _____
_____
_____

I've got a younger brother called Carl and a stepbrother, Sam. Even though Sam's my stepbrother and he's ten years older, we're quite close. He's at university now but we keep in touch and we sometimes go to football matches. Carl, on the other hand, is spoilt. He doesn't get into trouble, even when he's done something wrong, and he never does anything like emptying the dishwasher or clearing the plates away after a meal. I had to help in the house at his age. It's not fair!

Karen

Twins reunited

1 Read the profile of Martin Olsson and write a paragraph about him and his family.

Martin Olsson

Footballer

Name: Martin Tony Waikwa Olsson

Nationality: Swedish

Date of birth: 17th May, 1988

Place of birth: Gävle, Sweden

Parents: mother Kenyan, father Swedish

Siblings: older sister, Jessica (an art gallery director); identical twin brother Marcus (a footballer).
Jessica is married to basketball player Dirk Nowitzki.
They have two children, a boy called Max and a girl called Malaika.

Current teams: Norwich City Football Club, Swedish national football team

2 Read the study skills box and check what you have written in Exercise 1.

> **Writing: checking your work**
>
> Make sure that:
> - each sentence begins with a capital letter
> - each sentence ends with a punctuation mark
> - capital letters are used correctly, e.g. for days, months and nationality
> - the subject and the verb agree.
> - words are spelled correctly
> - each sentence makes sense.

Study skills

Martin Olsson is a (nationality and sport) _____.

(full name) *His full name* _____.

(date of birth, place of birth) *He was born* _____.

(parents) _____

(siblings) _____

(in-laws, nephews and nieces) _____

_____

3 Answer these questions about yourself.

1 Where were you born? _____

2 Where did you grow up? _____

3 Have you got any brothers and sisters?

Yes	No
Do you look alike?	Do you take after anyone in your family?
Do you share any of the same interests?	In what ways?

4 Read what Rachel and Shelley say. Complete the sentences using *both*, *both of*, *neither of*, *each other*.

Rachel

Shelley and I are twins. We were born on 28th April. I go to a girls' school in Camden. I'm quite good at Maths and Science; they're my favourite subjects, but I like languages too. My mum is a musician and so is my dad but I'm not good at music. I've got lots of friends at school but I often text Shelley during the day. I like team sports and so does Shelley. I hate swimming, though!

Shelley

I go to a girls' school in Barnet. Like Rachel, I'm quite good at Maths and Science and I enjoy languages. My parents are musicians but I'm not musical. Although Rachel and I don't go to the same school, we keep in touch by text during the day. We're quite sporty but I don't like swimming.

1 Rachel and Shelley were _____ born on 28th April.

2 _____ them go to girls' schools.

3 _____ them are good at Maths and Science.

4 They _____ like languages.

5 _____ them is good at music.

6 They text _____ during the day.

7 _____ them likes swimming.

Well done!

1 Use the words in the tables to write complete verb phrases.

> **Remember**
>
> Some verbs are followed by *to* + infinitive and some are followed by the *-ing* form. Some verbs also need a preposition:
>
> *She **blamed** him **for leaving** the window open.*
>
> See Grammar Section page 112.

1 accuse		for	doing something
2 blame		of	do something
3 congratulate	someone	on	
4 forgive		to	
5 remind			

6 apologise	about	doing something
7 complain	for	do something
8 insist	on	
9 offer	to	

10 deny	doing something
11 recommend	
12 suggest	

1 *accuse someone of doing something* _____

2 _____

3 _____

4 _____

5 _____

6 _____

7 _____

8 _____

9 _____

10 _____

11 _____

12 _____

2 Read the text in the speech balloons and report what the people said using the verbs in the boxes in Exercise 1.

1

> It's your fault, Peter. You shouldn't have left the window open.

Maggie

Maggie blamed Peter for leaving the window open.

2

> You took my bicycle without asking!

Jamie

_____

_____

> No, I didn't!

Ben

_____

_____

3

> I'm sorry I didn't reply to your message, Megan.

Joe

_____

_____

4

> Why don't we go for a walk by the river?

Saskia

_____

_____

5

> Don't forget to take your sports kit to school, Oliver.

Mum

_____

_____

6

> Well done for getting such a brilliant result in the exam, Malik!

Anita

_____

_____

7

> Shall I make you a sandwich, Jessica?

Miranda

_____

_____

8

> Philip, don't worry about losing my football. We're still friends!

Robel

_____

_____

9

> I've got too much homework to do.

Givence

_____

_____

Personal appearance

All dressed up

1 How many compound adjectives can you make from the words in the two circles?

short
tight
knee
high
ankle
long

sleeved
fitting
heeled
length

long-sleeved

_____

_____

2 Now think of a garment which each of the compound adjectives can describe.

a long-sleeved blouse

_____

_____

3 Put the letters in the correct order to describe the objects.
Clue: they're all compound adjectives which don't have hyphens.

1 A slice of  d o m e h a m e cake.

2 A pair of  d a n d h a m e shoes.

3 A practical t r o w f r o a p e jacket that keeps you dry in all kinds of weather.

4 Look at the pictures and complete the text with the words and phrases from the box.

long-sleeved jacket	formal occasions	is worn	long socks
ankle-length	handmade belt	scarves	at the waist
highly patterned	handmade boots	-length	colour

Traditional dress in Bhutan

The ancient kingdom of Bhutan is situated high in the Himalayas. One of the most distinctive features of the Bhutanese people is their national dress.

   Men wear a *gho*, a [1]knee_____ robe. It's like a kimono. It's tied
[2]_____ by a traditional [3]_____. On their feet
they wear [4]_____ with shoes or traditional [5]_____ with
beautiful designs. For [6]_____ a long silk scarf, like a sash, is also worn.
It [7]_____ from the left shoulder to the right hip. The [8]_____ of the
scarf depends on your status. White is the colour for ordinary citizens.
   Women wear an [9]_____ dress, made from brightly coloured and
[10]_____ fabric. They wear a [11]_____
over the dress. Like the men, they wear long [12]_____ for formal occasions.

My style

1 What's just happened? Write a caption for each picture, following the model.

1   He's had his trousers repaired.

2 _____

3 _____

4 _____

5 _____

6 _____

2 Change the underlined noun into an adjective to complete each sentence.

1 He's got a great sense of <u>style</u>. He always looks very _____ .

2 Oh dear! This jumper looks like a <u>bag</u> on me. It's much too _____ .

3 If you're looking for <u>comfort</u>, choose silk. It's a very _____ material to wear.

4 You don't have to follow <u>fashion</u> to be _____ .

3 Complete the sentences with a suitable word.

1 We're going to my sister's wedding tomorrow, so we've all got to get dressed _____ .

2 She's always wearing the latest styles. She's very fashion-_____ .

3 Loose-fitting jackets aren't fashionable any more. People prefer _____-fitting jackets.

4 I'm not keen on wearing bright colours. I prefer _____ shades like pale blue and pale green.

5 I don't mind wearing smart clothes for special occasions but I'm much happier when I'm wearing _____ clothes.

4 Complete the conversation with suitable verbs in the –ing form.

Mum: Come on, Alex. We've got to buy you some new clothes and shoes.

Alex: Oh, Mum, [1]_____ for clothes is not my favourite weekend activity. What I enjoy is [2]_____ into town to meet my friends.

Mum: Yes, I know but you've got the interview for your new school on Monday morning. Now, come on.

Alex: [3]_____ dressed up is not my idea of fun.

Mum: Yes, but [4]_____ smart and well-dressed is important. You need to make a good impression. I know you like [5]_____ jeans and a T-shirt all day but on Monday it will be important to look smart.

Alex: I suppose so. But [6]_____ on clothes on a Saturday afternoon, how boring is that? I don't mind [7]_____ at clothes online, Mum.

Mum: But you can't try things on. Anyway, let's treat ourselves to a pizza at Da Mario's afterwards.

Alex: Oh yes! One of my favourite weekend activities is [8]_____ a pizza.

Mum: I thought it might be.

A fashion classic

Football fashion – the early years

The first football clubs were formed in England in the mid-nineteenth century. There were no club kits but players wore caps, scarves or sashes of the same colour over the white shirts and trousers that they wore when they were playing cricket.

The first reference to team colours comes from the rules of Sheffield Football Club, in 1857: "Each player must provide himself with a red and dark blue flannel cap."

The first club kits began to appear around 1870. Before that time, it was often hard to tell which side a player was on. In the first FA Cup final in 1872, the Wanderers team wore pink, black and cerise (deep pink), while their opponents, the Royal Engineers, played in red and navy (dark blue) shirts. At this time in England, the game was played by men from the upper and upper middle classes. They could afford to buy a shirt in their club's colours from their tailor. In

Scotland, however, football was taken up by the working classes during the 1870s.

In 1879, Darwen, a team of cotton mill workers from the north of England, met the upper class team of the Old Etonians in the FA Cup semi-final. The mill workers were laughed at for wearing trousers which had been cut off half way down the leg to make them knee-length. The Old Etonians wore expensive specially-made baggy trousers called 'knickerbockers', which also came down to just below the knee.

Players' tops were known as 'jerseys' (close-fitting, long-sleeved, knitted garments without a collar). Players who were chosen to play for their county or the international team often had a badge sewn onto their jerseys.

By the end of the nineteenth century, most of the leading clubs were wearing club kits that are similar to those they wear today, and football had become a game of the working classes.

1 Read the article *Football fashion – the early years.* Answer the questions.

1 How many words can you find for items of clothing? Write them here.

_____

_____

2 How many words can you find for colours? Write them here.

_____

3 Which two words are used to describe shades of colour?

_____

4 Which word describes a type of cloth usually made of cotton or wool? _____

5 Which word describes a person who makes clothes? _____

6 Which word describes something you can sew onto your football kit? _____

2 Read the article again. Then answer these questions.

1 Which period does the article cover? _____

2 Why did different clubs start to have their own team colours? _____

_____

3 Why do you think people laughed at what the Darwen team players were wearing in the 1879 FA Cup semi-final? _____

_____

_____

3 In your notebook, write a paragraph describing what this modern-day footballer is wearing.

He's wearing a short-sleeved …

Study tip

Think before you write!

Before writing this paragraph, think of:

- the shirt (sleeves, fit)
- what is on the shirt (logo, badge)
- the shorts (length)
- what is on the shorts (number)
- socks (length).

Moods and feelings

Ups and downs

1 Solve the crossword.

Across

1 Extremely happy about something. (8)

4 I can always find something to do. I'm never _____. (5)

9 I'm going skiing for the first time. I'm a bit _____ but I know I'll enjoy it. (12)

10 Extremely frightened. (9)

11 I was very _____ when I heard I'd been chosen for the football team. (7)

12 Sad because something was not as good as you expected. (12)

Down

2 Mixed up. (8)

3 Extremely angry. (7)

5 I often get _____ before a football match, but as soon as I'm on the field I feel OK. (7)

6 Sad or worried when something bad has happened. (5)

7 Very pleased. (9)

8 Feeling very down and miserable. (9)

Language tip

absolutely and very with adjectives

Some of the adjectives for emotions are 'extreme': *furious, ecstatic, terrified.*

Some adjectives for emotions are 'degree' adjectives: *annoyed, happy, frightened.*

You can be *a bit annoyed* (a degree adjective) but you can't be *a bit furious* (an extreme adjective).

You can make these adjectives stronger. Use *absolutely* with extreme adjectives: *absolutely furious, absolutely ecstatic, absolutely terrified.*

Use *very* with degree adjectives: *very annoyed, very happy, very frightened.*

For lists of extreme adjectives and degree adjectives, see Grammar Unit 3 on page 113.

2 Complete these sentences to describe how you yourself would (or wouldn't) feel in these situations. Remember you can use *very* and *absolutely*.

1 If somebody borrowed one of my things without asking first,
I'd feel _____ / *I wouldn't feel* _____

2 If my favourite football team played really well and won a match against a top team,
_____

3 If I'd got nothing to do, my friends were all away for the weekend and it was too hot to go out,
_____

4 If I'd just watched a very frightening film and there was a power cut so all the lights went out,
_____

5 If the headteacher asked me to recite a poem from memory in front of the whole school,
_____

3 Look at the pictures and complete the sentences using *must have / might have / can't have*.

What must have happened?	**What might have happened?**	**What can't have happened?**
1 Where are my keys ? Oh no, I _____ _____ _____ _____ _____ _____ _____	**2** I thought I'd put my phone in my pocket, but I _____ _____ _____ _____ _____ _____	**3** I've only just bought you a new watch. You _____ _____ _____ _____ _____ _____

Problems and solutions

1 Replace the phrases in italics with the expressions from the box in the correct form.

calm down	fall out with	
catch up	make up	put (something) behind you
cheer up	move on	

Anya: You look anxious. What's on your mind?

          1 _____ *I fell out with* _____
                 ↓

Sophie: Well, *I had an argument with* my best friend on Monday and I feel really bad about it.

Anya: What was it about?

Sophie: She was getting really upset about missing some lessons and she was worried

         2 _____
              ↓

that she wouldn't be able to *do the work she'd missed* before the end of term. I told her

   3 _____
      ↓

to *relax and not be so emotional*. But that made her worse and she really shouted at me.

Anya: Well why don't you just act normally, as if nothing had happened?

       4 _____
          ↓

Sophie: It's not as easy as that. You can't just *forget all about something like that*.

            5 _____
               ↓

Anya: Maybe the thing to do then is to apologise and tell her you want to *be friends again*.

     6 _____
         ↓

Sophie: You're probably right. We need to *go forward* now.

    7 _____
        ↓

Anya: You're right. Come on. *Try to be happy again*. Let's see a smile!

2 Circle the correct option in each sentence.

1 It's wrong to talk about someone behind their *back / face*.

2 I know you didn't mean to get angry. Don't feel *bad / wrong* about it.

3 It must have been difficult to tell the headteacher what happened but you did the *good / right* thing.

4 When you're *in the wrong / in the wrong way*, the best thing to do is to apologise.

5 When you've had an argument with a friend and you want to make up, it's sometimes hard to *do / make* the first move.

6 If you want to be in the school play you should go to the audition. You've got nothing to *lose / miss*.

7 You're looking worried. What's on your *head/ mind*?

8 It's not always my fault but I always *get / have* the blame.

9 It's no use giving her advice. It's not going to *make / do* any difference because she'll do what she wants to do anyway.

10 I think you've got the wrong *impression / expression* of him. He's a really nice person.

3 Write captions for these cartoons using *always* and the present continuous.

1

(buy / new shoes) *She's always* _____

_____

_____

3

(Those tourists / drop / litter) _____

_____

_____

2

(They / go / on holiday) _____

_____

_____

4

(They / play / loud music) _____

_____

_____

Beyond words

1 Read the text and find the words for the following:

1 movements with the hand, arm or head to show what you're thinking or feeling

_____

2 spending time enjoying yourself with other people

_____

3 continuing for a long time

_____

4 ready to argue or make someone angry

_____

5 completely unacceptable

_____

6 openness to new ideas and suggestions

_____

2 Make abstract nouns from these adjectives.

1 friendly _____*friendliness*_____

2 embarrassed _____

3 impatient _____

4 confused _____

5 insane _____

6 receptive _____

7 confident _____

3 Decide whether the following words are adjectives or nouns. Write *adj* or *n* next to them.

1 silent _____

2 offence _____

3 culture _____

4 aggressive _____

It's important to know which gestures are appropriate and which are not when, for example, you're greeting people and socialising. In some countries, you should avoid sustained eye contact in order to avoid appearing confrontational. In other cultures, you should be aware that it is taboo to touch someone's head, even if they're a child.

When you're in conversation with someone, it's important to know how to show receptiveness to what they're saying. In some countries this can be shown by silence and in others, you're expected to say that you agree with them.

Dictionary work

Using a dictionary can really help you improve your language skills. Here, for example, you can see how the two different adjectives, *embarrassed* and *embarrassing*, are used and how the verb and the noun are used.

embarrass /ɪmˈbærəs/ **verb**
to make someone feel ashamed or shy: *My dad's always embarrassing me in front of my friends.*

embarrassed /ɪmˈbærəst/ **adj**
B1 feeling ashamed or shy: *I was too embarrassed to admit that I was scared.*

embarrassing /ɪmˈbærəsɪŋ/ **adj**
B1 making you feel embarrassed: *I forgot his name – it was very embarrassing.*

embarrassment /ɪmˈbærəsmənt/
noun [no plural]
shy, ashamed, or uncomfortable feelings: *He blushed with embarrassment.*

If you look up *embarrassed* in the dictionary you will see that it is an adjective.

You will also see an example of how to use it in a sentence.

In addition, you can see that there is a verb, *embarrass*, another adjective, *embarrassing*, and a noun, *embarrassment*.

Source: *Cambridge Essential English Dictionary*, CUP 2011

4 Look up the words in Exercise 3 in a dictionary and answer these questions.

1 For each adjective, is there a corresponding noun? What is it? _____

2 For each noun, is there a corresponding adjective? What is it? _____

3 Does your dictionary tell you how to use the words you looked up in context?
If so, write some examples here.

_____

_____

_____

5 Circle the correct option in each sentence.

1 There was absolute *silent / silence / silently* in the room. You could have heard a pin drop.

2 Tapping your finger on the side of your head can be *offence / offensive / offend* in some cultures.

3 You can learn a lot about the *culture / cultural / culturally* of another country by listening to its music.

4 It's better to listen patiently, even when you disagree with someone, than to express yourself in an *aggression / aggressive / aggressively* way.

4 The world of music

What does music mean to you?

1 Put the letters in the correct order to complete what the people are saying.

1 **"**I've got a guitar and I'm starting to write my own

   (s g o n s) _____.**"**

2 **"**I know the (e n u t) _____ but I can't remember the
   words.**"**

3 **"**My favourite (s l i c a l a c s) _____ piece of music is Vivaldi's
   Four Seasons.**"**

4 **"**She's both a musician and a writer. She not only writes her own music, she also
   writes her own (r i c y l s) _____.**"**

5 **"**His music is quite sad but it suits the (l a b l a d s) _____
   he writes. **"**

6 **"**Spanish flamenco music has a strong and distinctive

   (t h y r m h) _____. It's called the *compás*.**"**

2 Complete the abstract noun in each sentence.

1 Her father had played first violin in the orchestra and it was a great
   *consol*_____ to her to be able to hear the recordings of him playing.

2 She listened in *won*_____. It was the first time she'd been to an orchestral concert.

3 Hearing the music again filled him with *nostal*_____.

4 Although the symphony started with a series of loud drum beats, it ended with a great
   sense of *peaceful*_____.

5 The first movement of the piece was quite loud and aggressive but it had its moments
   of *tender*_____.

6 The music at the end of the opera reflects the *sad*_____ and the
   *distr*_____ of the main character as she faces her loss.

3 Every seventh word in each of these texts is missing.
Write a suitable word in each gap.

- Some may be simple words like *a* or *to*.
- There can be several possibilities for some of the gaps.

What does music mean to you, Saskia?

I love music because it expresses [1]_____ lot of the things I feel. [2]_____ I listen to a song about [3]_____ with friends and having a good [4]_____ , it makes me feel happy. I [5]_____ to sad songs too and perhaps [6]_____ I'm a bit down, they make [7]_____ feel better, not so alone. For [8]_____ it's important that a song has [9]_____ good tune because it makes me [10]_____ to sing it.

What does music mean to you, Khalid?

If I'm having a bad day [11]_____ can really help to chill out [12]_____ listen to some music. It doesn't [13]_____ to be a song with words, [14]_____ can be any kind, such as [15]_____ , guitar, bass, a jazz band or [16]_____ you like best! But for me, [17]_____ needs to have a strong beat. [18]_____ like to move to music. It [19]_____ me feel more alive. Music means [20]_____ lot to me.

4 Report what Liam said. Use the present tense but remember to make the necessary changes, as in the example.

Liam

1 I live for music. Playing music is like breathing for me.
Liam said <u>he lives</u> for music. Playing music is like breathing for <u>him</u>.

2 I like music that reflects my mood.

_____

3 I don't listen to jazz because I don't really like it.

_____

4 Of all the classical composers, I like Mozart best.

_____

5 My brother's favourite instrument is the piano but mine is the guitar.

_____

West meets East through music

1 Solve the crossword.

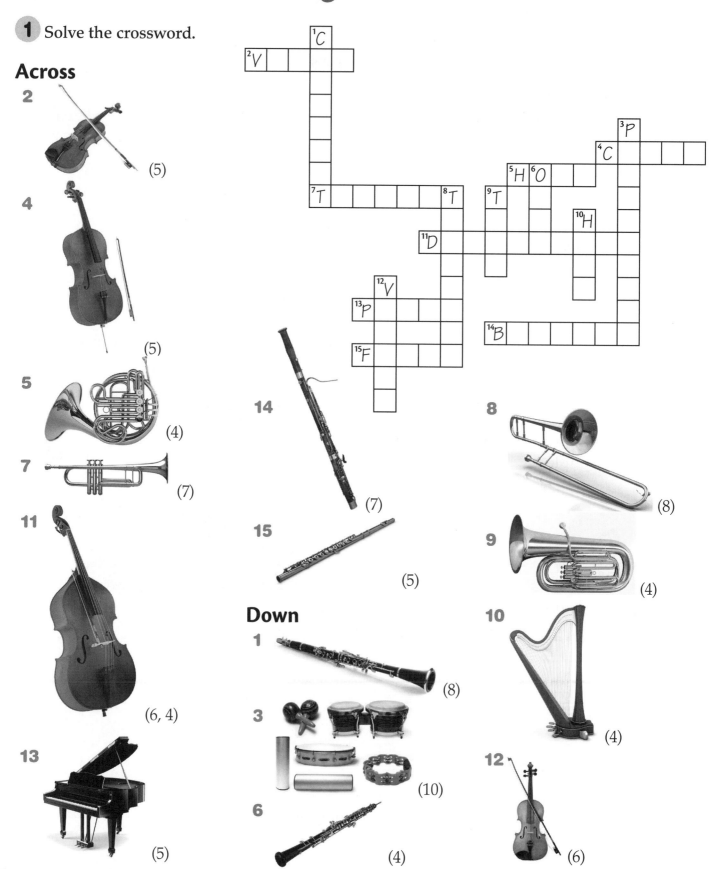

Across

2 (5)

4 (5)

5 (4)

7 (7)

11 (6, 4)

13 (5)

14 (7)

15 (5)

8 (8)

9 (4)

10 (4)

Down

1 (8)

3 (10)

6 (4)

12 (6)

2 A young violinist phones you to ask about the summer workshop and tour of the West-Eastern Divan Orchestra. Use the notes to answer her questions.

Violinist: I'm a violinist and I'd like to find out about the summer workshop and tour. Can you tell me when it is?

You: _____

_____

Violinist: Is the tour only in Europe?

You: _____

_____

Violinist: I'm only 15. Am I old enough to audition?

You: _____

Violinist: And what do I have to do to audition?

You: _____

_____

_____

West-Eastern Divan Orchestra

Summer workshop and tour

Dates: July 24 – August 19
Location: Argentina, Germany, Switzerland, Austria and UK
Age range: 14–28

To audition:
video recording, 10 minutes
(audio recording not acceptable)
CV + application form

Promenade Concert:
West-Eastern Divan Orchestra
and Daniel Barenboim

Tuesday 18th August, 19.30

Royal Albert Hall

A varied programme including the Beethoven Triple Concerto for violin, cello and piano. Soloists: Guy Braunstein (violin), Kian Soltani (cello), Daniel Barenboim (piano).

3 Read the concert programme and write questions for these answers.

1 Who _____

The West-Eastern Divan Orchestra and Daniel Barenboim.

2 _____

On Tuesday 18th August.

3 _____

At half-past seven in the evening.

4 _____

At the Royal Albert Hall.

5 _____

Guy Braunstein, Kian Soltani and Daniel Barenboim.

The sound of music

1 Link the two halves of the questions.

1	Who invented the phonautograph, a device	**a** become a thing of the past?
2	How	**b** by 1929?
3	What was the earliest	**c** did the phonautograph work?
4	What could Thomas Edison's phonograph	**d** do?
5	Who invented	**e** for recording sound?
6	What had happened	**f** of stereo sound?
7	Who	**g** recording of the human voice?
8	Why did acoustic recordings	**h** the gramophone?
9	What was the main advantage	**i** 'Talking Books' introduced?
10	When were the first	**j** was Enrico Caruso?

2 Here are the answers to six of the questions in Exercise 1. What are the questions?

Question 1: *2c How did the phonautograph work?*

Answer: It traced the shape of sound waves on smoke-blackened paper or glass.

Question 2: _____

Answer: A song called *Au clair de la lune*.

Question 3: _____

Answer: Flat discs had taken over from cylinders.

Question 4: _____

Answer: He was an opera singer and the first superstar recording artist.

Question 5: _____

Answer: It gave a wider field of sound.

Question 6: _____

Answer: In 1934.

3 Read the text on page 27 and answer the questions.

1 What is this text about? _____

_____

2 Where might you find it? _____

3 Why does the writer include what some people actually said at the time? _____

_____

'Wait a minute! Wait a minute! You ain't heard nothing yet!' declared Al Jolson to an enthralled cinema audience, but almost nothing could be heard above the cheering and clapping. The audience were delighted. They had just heard the first words ever spoken in a feature fiction film.

It was 1927 and the opening night of *The Jazz Singer* in New York. Al Jolson's words were to prove prophetic. Once the technology had been developed to synchronise sound to film, the era of silent movies was over. Audiences around the world were thrilled by the introduction of sound, which brought a new realism to the movies. 'We felt we were really there when we could hear it,' says Kathleen Green, who saw *The Jazz Singer*

when it was first screened in Britain. The idea of talking movies was so revolutionary that some people just could not believe they existed. 'We told my grandmother about the film when we came back,' Kathleen Green remembers, 'and she would not have it. Absolutely not ... she would not believe you could hear them talking.'

The first sound systems were primitive yet highly effective, giving films a completely new dimension that could be used in many ways. Lisetta Salis, who went with her friends to see the film when it came to her hometown in Italy, remembers the effect it had on them all. 'We kept saying to one another, "Let's watch it again".' And they did.

4 Find these words in the text. Use the context to try to understand them. In your notebook, write down what you think each one means. Then check your answers in a dictionary.

1 enthralled

2 prophetic

3 synchronise

4 screened

5 revolutionary

6 primitive

Understanding meaning from context

Study skills

You can sometimes get close to what a word means from clues in the sentence in which it occurs. Look at 'enthralled', for example, at the beginning of the first paragraph. What does it mean? We know it describes the cinema audience and we know that they were very happy because they were cheering and clapping. They were delighted by what they had seen and heard. So we know that 'enthralled' describes the positive feeling the audience had to what they were seeing and hearing. In fact, the dictionary definition of 'enthralled' is 'so interested in or excited by something that you give it all your attention'.

5 Look back at the text and answer these questions.

1 Al Jolson said, 'You ain't heard nothing yet!' What did he mean?

   a The sound isn't working yet.

   b This is just the beginning. There's a lot more to come.

   c You've never heard a film with sound before.

2 Why were Al Jolson's words prophetic? _____

5 Health and diseases

A game changer

1 Rewrite these sentences, replacing the words in italics with the verb phrases in the box.

cut down on	give up
cut out	keep up (with)
	snack on

1 Don't *eat* sweets and crisps *between meals*.

_____

_____

2 Just do your best in the race. Don't worry if you can't *go as fast as* the others.

_____

_____

_____

3 You need to *eat less* chocolate.

_____

_____

4 You need to *remove* sugary foods *from your diet*.

_____

_____

5 Don't *stop* swimming. It's a really good form of exercise.

_____

_____

_____

_____

2 Write the words for the definitions.

crisis   physically   energetic
collapse   fit   alert
pain   diet   mood
snack

1 _____: a small amount of food that is eaten between meals

2 _____: able to do a lot of physical things

3 _____: able to think and act quickly

4 _____: a situation which has reached an extremely difficult or dangerous point

5 _____: an unpleasant physical feeling caused by illness or injury

6 _____: fall down suddenly because you haven't got enough strength

7 _____: healthy and strong, especially as a result of exercise

8 _____: in a way that relates to the body

9 _____: mental and emotional state at a particular time

10 _____: the food that someone usually eats

3 Novak Djokovic changed his diet and it had a dramatic effect on his tennis. Read about three kinds of diet and look at the picture. Which diet does it relate to?

Three kinds of diet

The Mediterranean diet
The Mediterranean diet is southern European. It describes the kind of food people who live around the Mediterranean Sea eat. It features a lot of vegetables and fruit, both fresh and dried, as well as cereals, nuts and seeds. Olive oil is used for cooking. Cheese and yogurt are the main dairy foods. Moderate amounts of fish and poultry (chicken, etc) and small amounts of red meat are eaten.

The vegetarian diet
There are different kinds of vegetarian diets. There are lacto-vegetarian, ovo-lacto-vegetarian and even pesco-vegetarian diets.

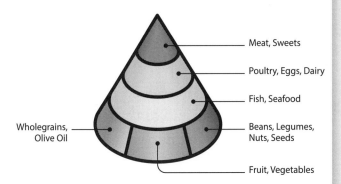

Meat, Sweets
Poultry, Eggs, Dairy
Fish, Seafood
Wholegrains, Olive Oil
Beans, Legumes, Nuts, Seeds
Fruit, Vegetables

The vegan diet
Unlike vegetarians, vegans do not eat anything that comes from an animal, including eggs, dairy products and honey. Vegans choose this diet not only for health reasons but also for environmental and ethical reasons.

4 Read the text again and read the Language tip. Then answer these questions.

1 What is a lacto-vegetarian?

_____

2 What is an ovo-lacto-vegetarian?

_____

3 What is a pesco-vegetarian?

_____

4 What ethical reasons might someone have for choosing a vegan diet?

_____

_____

_____

5 If you had guest who was a vegan, what would you give them for breakfast?

_____

_____

_____

Language tip

The prefix *lacto-* comes from the Latin *lac*, which means *milk*.

The prefix *ovo-* comes from the Latin *ovum*, which means *egg*.

The prefix *pesco-* comes from the Latin *piscis*, which means *fish*.

The word *ethical* comes from the Greek word *ethos*. The study of *ethics* is concerned with what is good and bad, right and wrong.

Food for thought

1 Solve the crossword.

Across

3 (*with 8 Across*) These are extremely small and can cause disease if they get into your body. (7)

5 The unit for measuring the amount of energy that food provides. (7)

7 A disease in which the body cannot control the level of sugar in the blood. (8)

8 (*with 3 Across*) These are also extremely small and can cause disease if they get into your body. (8)

10 The system that protects your body from illness. (6)

13 My grandparents always have breakfast at 9 o'clock, lunch at 1 o'clock and dinner at 7 o'clock. They believe that having _____ meals keeps you fit and healthy. (7)

14 It's a very common illness, especially in winter. (4)

16 The smallest living parts of an animal or plant. (5)

17 You find them in food and they give your body energy. (13)

Down

1 If you don't have a good diet and the right amount of sleep, you're more likely to be _____ to illness. (11)

2 Want something very much. (5)

4 A disease in a part of your body that is caused by *3 Across* or *8 Across*. (9)

5 Serotonin is a _____ which helps to keep your moods and emotions in balance. (8)

6 When you feel better again after an illness. (8)

9 It sends the blood around your body. (5)

11 It's important to eat a good breakfast to restore your blood _____ levels. (5)

12 Another word for disease. (7)

15 It's in your head and you can't think without it. (5)

2 Complete the phrases with the correct words from the list.

skip	infection	susceptible	protect	catch

1 to be _____ to infection

2 to _____ a cold

3 to _____ the immune system

4 to _____ a meal

5 to fight an _____

3 Use the phrases 1–5 in Exercise 2 to complete the following sentences.

1 Some health experts say that if you take vitamin C, you are less likely

_____

2 Your body needs a regular supply of food, which is why it is not a good idea

_____

3 Moderate exercise and a good diet help

_____

4 Doctors say that you should keep warm and drink plenty of liquids

_____ such as a heavy cold or flu.

5 Elderly people tend _____ more _____ than younger people.

4 Choose the appropriate word from the words in the circles to complete the text. (You will not need all of the words.)

Recent studies of diet and eating habits show that the number of overweight people in North America and in Europe is rapidly increasing. Being overweight can lead to serious health problems such as heart disease, diabetes and high blood pressure.

Doctors have a simple answer: eat [1] _____ _____ and exercise [2] _____ _____ .

(circle: more, less, healthy, healthily, regular, regularly)

According to leading educationalists, children who exercise regularly often do better at school, sleep [3] _____, are [4] _____ _____ to be overweight and are [5] _____ than [6] _____ _____ children. Another important consequence of doing exercise is that it helps to relieve stress and improve your mood.

However, giving advice is one thing, but getting people to follow it is another.

(circle: less, good, likely, better, stronger, active)

The story of vaccination

1 Complete this summary of the early history of the fight against smallpox using the prepositions from the box.

against	into	on x 3
from	of x 2	to x 3

Lady Mary Wortley Montagu saw how infected material was taken [1]_____ someone with smallpox. It was rubbed [2]_____ scratches made on the children's arms and it gave them immunity. She was so impressed that she persuaded doctors to test the method [3]_____ six prisoners. Later, one of the prisoners was exposed [4]_____ two children with smallpox and he was found to be immune [5]_____ the disease.

Edward Jenner had been inoculated [6]_____ smallpox when he was a boy, and he inoculated his own patients despite being aware [7]_____ the risks.

Jenner noticed that cowpox was similar [8]_____ smallpox, but not serious or fatal, and in 1796 he carried out an experiment [9]_____ an 8-year-old boy. He also tested the process [10]_____ his 11-month-old son. Edward Jenner's use of cowpox provided immunity without risk [11]_____ infection.

2 Complete each sentence with a word from the list and the appropriate preposition.

experiments	exposing	risks	similar	taken

1 Alligators are _____ _____ crocodiles but their heads are a different shape.

2 Several of the ideas in the film *Pirates of the Caribbean* are _____ _____ the adventure story, *Treasure Island*.

3 Visits to the cave paintings at Altamira in Spain are carefully controlled because it is feared that _____ them _____ light will damage them.

4 Gregor Mendel carried out _____ _____ pea plants, which was the basis of our understanding of genetics.

5 The scientist Marie Curie, who won the Nobel Prize for discovering radium and polonium, was not aware of the _____ _____ radiation.

3 Rewrite the sentences using the prompts.

1 Lady Mary Wortley Montagu was impressed by what she saw in Turkey. (*be / a very good idea*)
Lady Mary Wortley Montagu thought that what she saw in Turkey was a very good idea.

2 Smallpox was often fatal. (*die*)

_____

3 All the prisoners survived. (*die*)

_____

4 The prisoners were released. (*give / their freedom*)

_____

5 Despite the success of inoculation, there were still risks. (*Even though*)

_____

6 Inoculated people were temporary carriers of smallpox. (*for a time*)

_____

7 The carriers could infect others with the disease. (*pass on*)

_____

8 Inoculations with cowpox provided immunity from smallpox. (*protect / people*)

_____

4 Write a short biography of one of your parents, your grandparents or another relative. Use as many of the time expressions as you can.
My grandmother and grandfather were married in … . At first, they lived in …

Time prepositions:			Time adverbial phrases:	
in	at	from … to …	at first	over (a year) later
during	for	on	(two) months later	the following year
after	between … and …	since	shortly afterwards	many years later
by		until	last (year)	in his / her later years

_____

_____

_____

_____

_____

_____

_____

_____

6 Leisure time

Leisure for pleasure

1 Write a verb that can go before each of the nouns.

1 a mobile phone _____ *use a mobile phone / talk on a mobile phone* _____

2 the internet _____

3 TV _____

4 the radio _____

5 computer games _____

6 digital photos _____

7 a daily newspaper _____

2 Put these adverbs in order of frequency starting with the most frequent.

hardly ever   sometimes   never   often   always   almost always

_____

3 Write seven sentences about yourself combining the phrases you made in Exercise 1 with the adverbs in Exercise 2.

Example: I almost always use a mobile phone. I hardly ever use a landline.

_____

_____

_____

_____

_____

_____

_____

4 Write what these people might say about their interests. Be as imaginative as you like.

1 a film buff   (science fiction)   (comedy)   (favourites)   (scripts)

I enjoy watching all kinds of movies, from science fiction to comedy. I watch my favourites over and over again and I can remember quite a lot of the lines from the scripts.

2 a football fan

 support

 home matches, away matches

posters

_____

_____

3 a fitness fanatic

 sports centre

all kinds of sport

 athletics

_____

_____

4 a music lover

 download

concerts

 musical instruments

_____

_____

5 Write questions and answers about the survey. For the answers, choose from the phrases in the list.

None of them.	Quite a few.
Very few.	A lot.
Hardly any.	Almost all of them.
Not many.	All of them.

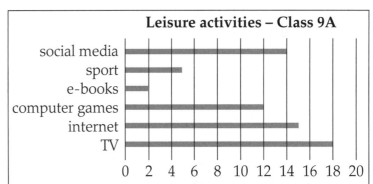

Leisure activities – Class 9A

The chart shows the results of a survey about the leisure time of students in Class 9A. The students were asked which activities they did every day.

1 Q: *How many of the students use social media every day?* _____

   A: *Quite a few.* _____

2 Q: _____

   A: _____

3 Q: _____

   A: _____

4 Q: _____

   A: _____

5 Q: _____

   A: _____

6 Q: _____

   A: _____

Finding time

1 Complete the conversation with suitable verbs. Remember to use the *-ing* form.

Harvey: Do you feel like [1]_____ to that new campsite near the beach this weekend?

Brandon: Camping? You must be joking. I can't stand [2]_____ on hard ground.

Harvey: What about you, John?

John: Well, I quite fancy [3]_____ to the beach but I don't really want to sleep in a tent. I don't mind [4]_____ in a youth hostel, though.

Brandon: I agree. Anyway, who wants to waste time [5]_____ up a tent?

Harvey: We can take some food and cook our own meals.

Brandon: Oh no, I can't face [6]_____ a meal after a hard day swimming and playing beach volleyball.

John: That's OK because I don't mind [7]_____ a meal as long as you do the washing up afterwards.

Brandon: Oh no, I really hate [8]_____ the washing up!

Harvey: It's OK, Brandon, I'll do the washing up. You just enjoy yourself.

Brandon: Good. Sounds like a plan!

2 How do you feel about doing these things? Choose five of them and write sentences using the verbs from the box.

- put the rubbish out
- go to the supermarket
- tidy my room
- surf the internet
- play computer games
- watch sport on TV
- meet up with friends in town

don't mind hate	can't stand (sometimes / never) feel like	(really) enjoy (often /never) fancy	(often / never) waste time

_____

_____

_____

_____

_____

3 Every seventh word in the magazine article is missing. Write a suitable word in each gap.

- Some may be simple words like *a* or *at*.
- Contractions, such as *couldn't* (= *could not*), count as one word.
- There can be several possibilities for some of the gaps.

Jay's challenge was to spend a week without using his mobile phone or his laptop.

It started on Tuesday. I thought [1] _____ first that it would be easy [2] _____ I was wrong. As soon as [3] _____ turned off our devices, it felt [4] _____ . The first day was OK because [5] _____ was at school. But that evening, [6] _____ I'd done my homework, I felt [7] _____ bit lost. I missed being in [8] _____ with my friends. I didn't know [9] _____ to do.

The next day at [10] _____ , Wednesday, I heard other people talking [11] _____ a video they'd seen on YouTube. [12] _____ were laughing and joking but I [13] _____ take part in the conversation because [14] _____ hadn't seen it.

That evening I [15] _____ the usual amount of time doing [16] _____ homework but instead of checking my [17] _____ and going on SnapChat, I watched [18] _____ really good film on TV. With [19] _____ messages coming in, I was able [20] _____ give it all my attention.

On [21] _____ I played football straight after school. [22] _____ when I got home I felt [23] _____ relaxed. I even picked up a [24] _____ which I'd wanted to read for [25] _____ . I didn't really think about using [26] _____ phone.

4 How would you feel if you did Jay's challenge? In your notebook, write the answers to these questions.

1 What would you miss?

2 What would you dislike about it?

3 What would you like about it?

A good night's sleep

1 Solve the crossword. The answers are all verbs.

Across

2 *Give advice.* 'I _____ you to go home and rest,' said the doctor. (6)

3 *Examine something to make sure it is correct; look at something to see if anything has changed.* 'I'll _____ my email to see if that message you sent me has arrived.' (5)

4 *Say that something is true or is a fact although you cannot prove it.* 'Some medicines _____ to help you sleep but it's much better to change your lifestyle to get a better night's sleep.' (5)

7 *Make sure.* 'When you're in a hot climate, you should _____ that you drink plenty of water.' (6)

9 *Stay away from a situation or prevent it from happening in the future.* 'You should _____ sugary drinks if you want to be healthy,' said the nutritionist. (5)

10 *Make someone aware of a possible danger or problem.* 'Health experts now _____ parents of the dangers of allowing children unlimited access to media devices.' (4)

11 *Send someone or something away and not allow them or it to come back.* 'If you have negative thoughts you must try to _____ them from your mind,' said the psychologist. (6)

Down

1 *Show something that is surprising or that was previously unknown.* 'If I tell you, please don't _____ my secret to anyone.' (6)

3 *Say that something is not right or that you are annoyed about something.* 'If you ate a good breakfast you wouldn't _____ about being hungry during the morning,' said Mum. (8)

5 *Go in a particular direction or have a particular result.* 'Too much exposure to the sun can _____ to serious skin problems.' (4)

6 *Encourage something to happen or develop.* 'Regular exercise is known to _____ good health.' (7)

8 *Give money as a payment for something; use time doing something.* 'My advice is to _____ your time and your money wisely.' (5)

10 *Relax.* 'You need to _____ down after a busy day.' (4)

2 Complete the text using the prompts.

Melatonin and sleep

Melatonin is a chemical ¹_____

It tells your body ²_____

The production of melatonin ³_____

It is released in the evening ⁴_____

Its effect is to ⁵_____

However, we don't always do the right things to promote the production of melatonin

⁶_____

a and at night.	**c** make you sleepy.	**e** when it's time to sleep and when it's time to wake up.
b is controlled by exposure to light.	**d** or to ensure that it is released at the right time.	**f** which occurs naturally in the body.

3 Complete the sentences with suitable imperatives, such as *Allow* and *Don't read*.

What can you do to stimulate the production of melatonin during the day?

¹_____Allow_____ natural light to come into the place where you work or study.

²_____ time outside each day to get enough – but not too much – exposure to sunlight.

What can you do to stimulate the release of melatonin at night?

³_____ the room you sleep in is dark. The darker your room is, the better you'll sleep.

⁴_____ all devices such as computers and televisions because the light from screens can suppress the release of melatonin.

⁵_____ from a device which is back-lit, such as an iPad. Instead, use an e-reader which is not back-lit. Or read a printed book.

⁶_____ your smartphone before you go to sleep.

4 Re-read the texts you've completed in Exercises 2 and 3 and answer these questions in your notebook.

1 What is melatonin and why is it important?

2 Why should you spend time outside each day?

3 Why is it important to sleep in a dark room?

4 If you like reading in bed, why is it not a good idea to read from a back-lit device?

5 Why do you think it's a good idea to turn off your smartphone before you go to sleep?

A tropical paradise

1 Complete the captions for the pictures.

1

v _ _ _ _ _ o

2

r _ _ _ f _ _ _ _ t

3

s h _ _ _ s

4

w _ _ d l _ f _

5

n _ _ _ _ _ _ _ l p _ _ k

2 Rewrite the sentences starting with the words and phrases given.

1 All the birds I saw in the rainforest were absolutely beautiful.

Every one _of the birds I saw in the rainforest was absolutely beautiful._

2 The majority of Costa Rica's renewable energy comes from hydroelectric power stations.

Most _____

3 Several beaches were ideal for surfing.

Some _____

4 Fifteen per cent of the country's power comes from geothermal sources.

Some _____

5 We visited two volcanoes but they weren't active.

Neither _____

6 The country was so beautiful that I didn't want to leave.

It was such _____

3 Every seventh word in the interview is missing. Write a suitable word in each gap.

- Some may be simple words like *a* or *of*.
- There can be several possibilities for some of the gaps.
- If you can't decide what to put in one of the gaps, leave it and carry on.
  You can come back to it later.

Presenter: Costa Rica is a small country [1]_____ Central America with a population of [2]_____ 4.8 million. Samira has been there. [3]_____, tell us, why is Costa Rica [4]_____ an attractive place?

Samira: Costa Rica is [5]_____ tropical paradise with fantastic rainforests, amazing [6]_____ and some beautiful beaches. And every [7]_____ of the beaches I visited had [8]_____ special.

Presenter: It sounds lovely.

Samira: Some of [9]_____ beaches were fantastic for swimming, others [10]_____ better for surfing. Some were full [11]_____ shells and there were others with [12]_____ right down to the sand.

Presenter: And [13]_____ are quite a lot of national [14]_____, aren't there?

Samira: Yes, it's got a [15]_____: a hundred and twenty four national [16]_____ and there are other protected areas. [17]_____ total, that's about 25% of the [18]_____ country. And it's one of the [19]_____ countries in the world which is [20]_____ to be carbon-neutral within ten years.

4 Write answers to these questions.

1 What is a national park?

_____

2 What is a rainforest?

_____

3 What is wildlife? Give examples.

_____

4 What is hydropower?

_____

5 What is an active volcano?

_____

6 What is geothermal power?

_____

What does it mean to be green?

1 Complete the compound adjectives in these sentences.

1 This torch is powered by the sun. It is _____-powered.

2 This washing powder is _____-friendly. It is not dangerous to the environment.

3 Use _____-energy light bulbs to save electricity. They also save you money because they're _____-lasting than ordinary light bulbs.

4 This car uses very little fuel. It's one of the most _____-efficient models you can buy.

2 Put the labels in the correct places on the diagram of the school.

a biomass boiler   a micro-hydro generator   a network of water pipes   an insulated thermal tank   solar power

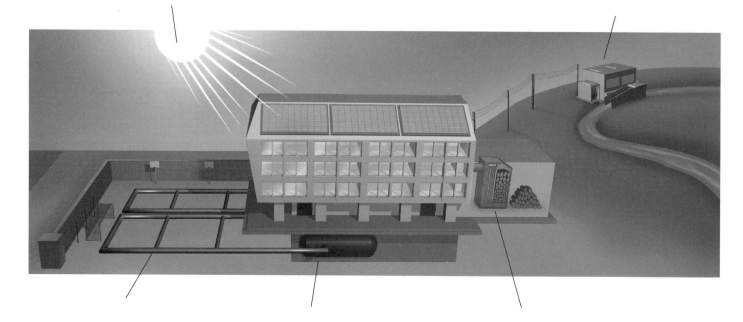

3 Write a description of the energy-efficient systems in the school above. Use the phrases from the box. Give as much detail as you can.

There are solar panels on the roof which ...	During the winter, heating is provided by ... and electricity is generated by ...	There is also a ...

_____

_____

_____

_____

_____

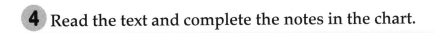
4 Read the text and complete the notes in the chart.

Go green, go to Reykjavik

Reykjavik, the capital of Iceland, is one of the world's greenest cities and an ideal eco-tourism destination.

The city is powered mostly by hydroelectricity and geothermal energy. Its buses are hydrogen-powered. You can rent ordinary or electric bikes and there are plenty of cycle paths, which make it easy to get around. It's also a pedestrian-friendly city if you want to walk.

You can stay in an eco-friendly hostel. You can relax in geothermally heated springs. Even though Iceland is in the Arctic circle, you can swim at a geothermal beach where the water is heated naturally. There are also geothermally heated swimming pools around the city.

Iceland is a great place for getting close to nature. You can go whale watching, and dolphins are often seen close to the coast. The Heidmork Nature Reserve is a great place to see wildflowers. There are trails for hiking and you can do day tours on horseback.

1 Sources of power	hydroelectricity, ...
2 Getting around in the city	
3 Accommodation	
4 Leisure activities	
5 Wildlife	

5 Answer these questions.

1 What is eco-tourism?

_____

2 What is a pedestrian-friendly city?

_____

3 What would you expect to find at an eco-friendly hostel?

_____

_____

_____

_____

The power of nature

1 Solve the crossword.

Across

1 *Look at the picture.* (9)

3 Uranium and plutonium are _____ fuels. (7)

6 *Look at the picture.* (3)

7 *Look at the picture.* It's not smoke, it's _____ . (5)

8 An adjective describing energy that replaces itself, so it never runs out (9)

10 A machine for producing electricity. (9)

11 Uranium and plutonium produce energy through a _____ reaction. (8)

12 *Look at the picture.* (4,7)

Down

2 Uranium is a _____ substance. (11)

4 They are a source of water power in the sea. (5)

5 *Look at the picture.* (5)

7 *Look at the picture.* (5, 5)

9 Coal, oil and natural gas are _____ fuels. (6)

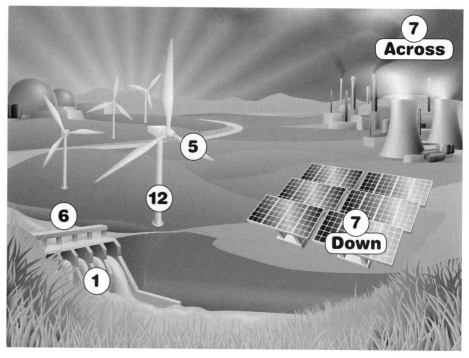

2 What are the advantages and disadvantages of the following?
Use the words in the box to help you.

clean / dirty	safe / dangerous	reliable / unreliable	renewable / non-renewable

nuclear power

1 *Nuclear power is* _____

However, _____

solar power

2 _____

_____

fossil fuels

3 _____

_____

wind power

4 _____

_____

wave power

5 _____

_____

3 What will life be like in 2050? Write a paragraph which includes the answers to these questions.

1 Where will you be living?

2 What kind of house will you be living in?

3 How will you be travelling around your town or city?

4 Where will you be working?

5 What will be the biggest change compared with life today?

_____

_____

_____

_____

_____

_____

_____

8 Industrial revolution

Water for food

1 Write the appropriate word for each of the following. The words are all in the box.

benefits	engineer	shallow	solution
canal	hydroponics	slopes	sustainable
crops	irrigation	soil	terraces

1 supplying land with water so that plants will grow _____

2 plants grown for food _____

3 a person who designs or builds machines, roads or bridges _____

4 flat areas cut out of the side of a hill or mountain and used for farming _____

5 the opposite of deep _____

6 the sides of a mountain _____

7 the material on the surface of the ground in which plants grow _____

8 a man-made waterway _____

9 a liquid into which a solid has been mixed and dissolved _____

10 a way of growing plants without soil _____

11 causing little or no damage to the environment and therefore able to continue for a long time _____

12 another word for 'advantages' _____

2 Choose from the words in the box in Exercise 1 to complete this text.

We can't grow major [1] _____ here, such as corn or vegetables or fruit, because the [2] _____ is very poor and there are no rivers or lakes nearby, so [3] _____ isn't an option. In other parts of the country, [4] _____ have been built on the [5] _____ of the mountains, so farmers have been able to grow olive trees and vines there. Here in the valley, however, we're starting to grow fruit, such as melons and strawberries, and vegetables, such as tomatoes and peppers, by a system called [6] _____. The plants are grown in a mineral [7] _____ rather than in the ground. The [8] _____ are that we can now grow food all year round and that we don't need a lot of water.

3 Choose the present passive or the past passive for the verbs in brackets to complete the text.

The story of the potato

More than five hundred years ago, before the arrival of the Spanish in South America, the Incas built terraces on the slopes of the Andes. They used them to grow crops such as potatoes. Canals [1] (*construct*) _were constructed_ to bring water from higher in the mountains to each terrace level. It [2] (*believe*) _____is believed_____ by historians today that around three thousand different kinds of potatoes [3] (*grow*) _____, to suit different types of soil and weather conditions. These terraces [4] (*still / use*) _____ today.

At the time of the Incas, it [5] (*think*) _____ that potatoes could be used to help people who were injured or ill. For example, slices of potato [6] (*put*) _____ on broken bones and they [7] (*rub*) _____ into the skin to help with skin problems.

Later it [8] (*find*) _____ that potatoes grew well in the Pyrenees, the mountains in northern Spain, and along the Atlantic coast of Spain. However, the Spanish didn't like potatoes much at first, and they weren't popular. But potatoes [9] (*take*) _____ to other countries in Europe and they [10] (*soon / find*) _____ to be useful for preventing famine when cereal crops failed due to bad weather conditions.

Check your tenses

It's easy to make mistakes in verb tenses, especially past and present tenses. Look for clues, such as time expressions, to tell you whether to use a present tense or a past tense.

past time   past passive

More than five hundred years ago ... Canals **were constructed** to bring water from higher in the mountains to each terrace level.

present passive   present time

It **is believed** by historians *today* that ...

Write two more past time expressions. (You'll find some in the text in Exercise 3.)
More than five hundred years ago

Can you think of some present time expressions?
Today

Full steam ahead!

1 The painting shows a famous inventor as a boy. Who is he? Solve the puzzle to find out.

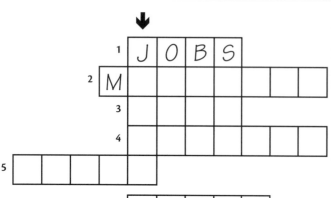
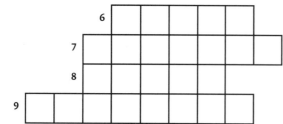

1 Children as young as six worked. They had _____ that started at 6 a.m. and finished at 7 p.m.

2 Workers were unhappy because _____ could do the work that they had been doing.

3 Coal is found in this place, deep under the ground.

4 In the eighteenth century, steam _____ were used for pumping water.

5 The early ones were powered by water. They produced cotton, paper and flour, for example.

6 The Ancient Egyptians used a water _____ to move water from low ground to high ground.

7 A building where things are made.

8 You get it when water boils.

9 Small houses for workers.

2 Why do you think the painter chose to show the boy looking at a steaming kettle?

_____

_____

_____

3 Every seventh word in this interview is missing. Write a suitable word in each gap.

- Some may be simple words like *a* or *it*.
- There can be several possibilities for some of the gaps.
- If you can't decide what to put in one of the gaps, leave it and carry on. You can come back to it later.

Presenter: Welcome to *The History Programme*. Today [1] _____*we're*_____ talking to Professor Johnson about the [2] _____ who worked in the mills at [3] _____ end of the eighteenth and the [4] _____ of the nineteenth centuries. What was [5] _____ like for these children?

Professor: It was [6] _____. Children as young as six years [7] _____ worked in the mills. They started [8] _____ 6 a.m. and finished at about 7 [9] _____ the evening. So they worked between [10] _____ and fourteen hours a day.

Presenter: Twelve [11] _____ fourteen hours a day! That can't [12] _____ been much fun for them. And [13] _____ many children worked in the mills?

Professor: [14] _____ lot. In some of Richard Arkwright's [15] _____, for example, two thirds of the [16] _____ who worked there were children.

4 Read the text in the box. Then complete the sentences below using the past perfect continuous, as in the example.

- For hundreds of years people worked at home spinning cotton. Then from 1740, factory owners started using spinning machines.
- Mine owners used Newcomen's steam engine to pump water out of mines for half a century. Then, in 1769, mine owners started using James Watt's more efficient steam engine.
- Engineers tried to use steam to power vehicles for several years but without success until Richard Trevithick produced the first steam train in 1804. It travelled a distance of 16 kilometres in 4 hours 5 minutes.
- People travelled between cities on horseback or in horse-drawn carriages. Everything changed from 1825 when the first railway line opened in Britain.

1 For hundreds of years before the invention of spinning machines in 1740, people _had been working at home spinning cotton._

2 Until James Watt invented a more efficient steam engine in 1769, mine owners _____
_____

3 Before Trevithick's steam train of 1804, engineers _____
_____

4 Everything changed in the years following the opening of the first railway line in Britain in 1825. Until then, people _____
_____

Can it or cool it!

1 These pictures show four ways of keeping food. Complete the words for each type of food.

1 f _ _ z _ n
2 r _ f _ _ g _ _ _ _ t _ d
3 t _ _ _ _ _ d
4 p r _ _ _ _ v _ d

2 What do these sentences mean? Choose the correct option.

1 *We take tinned food for granted now.*

   a Tinned food is cheap.

   b We think tinned food is old-fashioned.

   c Tinned food is not considered to be special.

2 *We buy our food daily from the market.*

   a We go to the market early to buy our food.

   b We go to the market every day to buy our food.

   c We go to the market once a week.

3 *Tinned food was in great demand.*

   a Lots of people wanted tinned food.

   b Tinned food was very expensive.

   c Food was only sold in large tins.

4 *The urban population was increasing.*

   a The number of people in the countryside was growing.

   b The number of wealthy people was growing.

   c The number of people in the cities was growing.

5 *The voyage was a triumph.*

   a The voyage was a disaster.

   b The voyage was a great success.

   c The voyage was very difficult.

3 Make one sentence from two using a relative pronoun each time: *who, which / that, where.* Write the sentences in your notebook.

1 Nicolas Appert was a chef. He won a prize for preserving food in sealed glass bottles.
   Nicolas Appert was a chef who won a prize for preserving food in sealed glass bottles.

2 Appert had a factory near Paris in the early 1800s. He preserved food such as vegetables, meat and dairy products there.

3 There's a new ice cream bar. You can get twenty-five different flavours of ice cream there.

4 Quinoa is a crop. It comes from South America.

5 Louis Pasteur was a French scientist. He invented a way of preserving milk and other foods by *pasteurisation*.

6 Archaeologists in China and Iraq have found the remains of ancient ice houses. They were used to store ice to preserve food.

4 Read the text. Which way of preserving food does it describe? _____

The Incas, who lived in the Andes in South America five hundred years ago, discovered a way of preserving potatoes. Raw potatoes are 80 per cent water. At night, the cold of the Andes froze them. During the day, however, they thawed in the warmth of the sun. As they defrosted, the workers stamped on them to press out all the moisture. After several days of alternating freezing and defrosting, the potatoes were dehydrated and transformed into a lightweight, transportable substance known as *chuno*. Stored in sealed, permanently frozen underground storehouses, the freeze-dried potatoes kept for five or six years. When needed, the *chuno* could be reconstituted by soaking in water and then cooked, or ground into flour, with no loss of nutritional value. *Chuno* was so precious to the Incas that it was used as currency.

5 Find the words for the following in the text and write them in the spaces.

1 uncooked _____

2 became warmer so that the ice melted and became water _____

3 became warmer and no longer frozen _____

4 lifted their feet and put them down again hard on the ground _____

5 very small amounts of water in a substance or in the air _____

6 two things happening one after the other, then the pattern is repeated _____

7 changed completely _____

8 not weighing much _____

9 changed back to the original condition _____

10 past particple of *grind*, broken into very small pieces or made into powder _____

11 very valuable _____

12 money used in a particular country _____

Facts and figures

1 Answer the questions.

Data quiz

These are examples of different kinds of data. What information does each one give? Where might you find them?

1 8 m²

This is a measurement. (It means '8 square metres') You might find it on a floor plan of a building.

2 dep. 20.00
arr. 21.30
These are ...

3

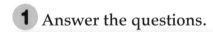

Nutrition Facts
Serving Size 5 oz. (144 g)
Servings Per Container 4

Vitamin A 1%	**Vitamin C** 2%
Calcium 2%	**Iron** 5%

This tells you...

4 b. 1882
d. 1945

5 00 34 972 5861

6 US$ 1 = ¥ 123

7 min. 5°C
max. 28°C

8 September 2016
19 Mon

9 50 km/h

2 Look at the graph and answer the questions:

1 What does the graph show? _____

_____

2 Which month is the hottest and which is the coolest?

_____

3 Is there a big difference between the highest and lowest temperature? Is the same true of the rainfall?

_____

_____

Mumbai

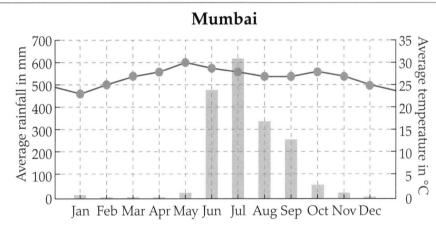

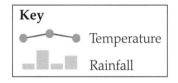

Key

Temperature

Rainfall

3 Use the information on the graph to complete this conversation.
Choose from the words in the box. You will not need all of them.

Tom: Which is the ¹ ____wettest____ month in Mumbai?

Leela: July, definitely. July has ² _____ rainfall than any other month.

Tom: And which is the ³ _____ month?

Leela: That's usually May. It can be 30 degrees – sometimes more.

Tom: Which months have the ⁴ _____ rainfall?

Leela: February, March and April.

Tom: Which is the ⁵ _____ popular month of year to visit?

Leela: February is a good time to go.

Tom: And when should you avoid going?

Leela: The ⁶ _____ popular month is July. ⁷ _____ people go in July than in any other
month, because it can be very hot and it's ⁸ _____ than any other month.

Tom: What about November?

Leela: Yes, November's OK, but there's ⁹ _____ rain in February than in November, so I'd go
in February.

Tom: OK. Thanks, Leela.

hot	hotter	hottest
wet	wetter	wettest
few	fewer	fewest
	more	most
	less	least

What are the facts?

Ban iPads in schools

Tom Bennett, an education expert, says that iPads should be banned in schools.

'Schools are increasingly giving kids iPads, even primary schools. I am not a fan of that. There is absolutely no research evidence that giving kids technology helps them learn ... Some people say, "Give kids iPads because they love them and then they'll love learning too." No, kids love iPads, that's all.'

According to Mr Bennett, rather than helping students to learn, gadgets such as iPads just distract them. Students use them to look at photos of celebrities and even to send each other insults online. He criticised parents who allow their children to stay up late using smartphones and tablets. He said that as a result, children arrive at school too tired to work.

Mr Bennett also said there is 'absolutely no need' for children to have access to the Internet and he was critical of teachers who tell children to use search engines to complete homework. He said it was like taking them to a library without a librarian.

1 Read the text and find the words for the following:

1 a person who knows a lot about a particular subject

_____

2 not allowed

_____

3 information that makes you believe that something is true

_____

4 small, useful and cleverly designed tools or machines

_____

5 make someone stop giving their attention to something

_____

6 words that are intended to hurt

_____

7 the person who helps you find information in a library

_____

2 Find these compound nouns in the text and write an explanation for each one.

1 education expert

_____

_____

_____

2 primary school

_____

_____

_____

3 research evidence

_____

_____

_____

4 search engine

_____

_____

_____

3 Read the statements. Write true or false.

According to Tom Bennett ...

1 iPads should only be used occasionally in schools. _____

2 Fewer schools are providing students with iPads than they were in the past. _____

3 Students love iPads because they help them learn. _____

4 Students' attention is taken away from their work by things they see on iPads. _____

5 Part of the blame rests with parents. _____

6 Students should only use the Internet when they're in a library. _____

4 In your notebook, write a short essay giving your response to the article _Ban iPads in schools_.

Paragraph 1 (Introduction)
Summarise Tom Bennett's opinions.

Paragraph 2
Say which points you agree with, giving your reasons.

Paragraph 3
Say which points you disagree with, giving your reasons.

Paragraph 4 (Conclusion)
Say what you think school policy should be on the use of iPads and other gadgets.

How to write an essay giving your point of view

Study skills

Don't just give your own opinions. Include the opinions of other people, especially experts.

Support what you say with reasons and examples. Include research evidence, such as results of surveys.

Your conclusion should reflect the opinions you've given.

In an essay, be careful about the way you give your opinions. Your argument will be stronger if you express your views in a logical and reasonable way. Don't write, for example, 'I think it's absolutely ridiculous that ...'. Instead write, 'It is not reasonable to say that ... '

What can numbers tell you?

1 Solve the crossword.

Across

2 A group of things that belong together. (3)

5 Another word for numbers. (7)

7 Information, especially facts or numbers. (4)

9 *Mode*, *median* and *mean* are three different kinds of _____. (7)

11 A series of related events, things or numbers that have a particular order. (8)

12 A mathematical word meaning 'take away' or 'minus'. (8)

Down

1 A mathematical expression meaning 'out of a hundred'. (3, 4)

3 Getting bigger, the opposite of *decreasing*. (10)

4 Half way between, in the _____. (6)

6 The science of using information discovered from studying numbers. (10)

7 A mathematical word meaning 'shared'. (7)

8 The number of times something happens. (9)

10 In statistics, this is the difference between the biggest and the smallest in a set of numbers. (5)

2 Complete these questions and answers.

1 Q: What is the next number in this _____ : 1, 2, 3, 5, 8, 13, ... ?

A: It's _____

2 Q: I got 7 out of 10 in the History test, so that's 70 per _____. And I got 18 out of 20 in the English test. What _____ is that?

A: It's _____

3 Q: What is special about this number square?

A: _____

_____

_____

4	9	2
3	5	7
8	1	6

3 Write the missing words to complete the dialogues.

A: Have you got the History test results?

B: Yes, I've got them here.

A: What was the highest mark?

B: The ¹_____ mark was nine and the ²_____ was two.

A: So nine minus two is seven.

B: OK, so that's the range.

A: Now we need to ³_____ up all the numbers.

B: I've already done that on the calculator. The ⁴_____ is: 120.

A: And there are 20 students in the class so that's a hundred and twenty ⁵_____ by twenty.

B: That's six. So that's the mean.

A: Next we need to write out the ⁶_____ in sequence and find the one in the middle.

B: OK, the number in the middle is six.

A: So the answer is six . And that's the median.

A: What's the ⁷_____ common mark, the mark most people got?

B: Well, that's five: there were seven people who got five marks.

A: OK, so that's the mode.

4 Solve the puzzle.

A pizza puzzle

- You have to cut this pizza into eight pieces.
- You can only use three cuts.
- One of the cuts isn't a straight line.
- The pieces don't have to be the same size.

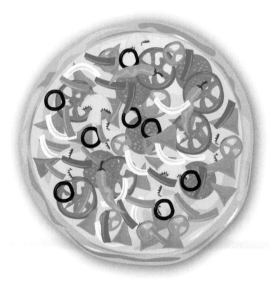

1 How would you cut it? Try to work it out. (The answer is on page 118.)

2 Write the instructions for cutting the pizza:
   *First cut the pizza ...*_____

   _____

   _____

   _____

   _____

3 Try the puzzle out on your friends and family.

Picture it!

1 These words all end in *-tion*. What are they?

1 A picture used for decorating or explaining something.   _____illustration_____

2 A formal talk in which you describe or explain something
to a group of people.   p r _ _ _ _ _ _ _ t i o n

3 Facts or details.   i n _ _ _ _ _ _ t i o n

4 Moving pictures.   a n _ _ _ _ t i o n

5 The process of changing from one form to another.   t r _ _ _ _ _ t i o n.

2 Look at the *Study skills* box and correct the mistakes in these sentences.

       subject

1 What is the <u>matter</u> of your presentation?   *v*

2 The way you present your material <u>depends of</u> your audience.   *gr*

3 Illustrate your talk with <u>graphs photos</u> and diagrams.   *p*

4 Don't use <u>to</u> many pictures.   *sp*

5 That's a great poster. Put <u>up it</u> on the wall.   *w.o.*

6 You want your listeners to <u>concentrate what</u> you're saying.   *∧*

> **Study skills**
>
> Some teachers use symbols to help you identify your mistakes.
>
> p   punctuation
> sp   spelling
> gr   grammar
> w.o. word order
> v   vocabulary
> ∧   there's a word missing.

3 Look at these four pieces of advice. Why are they important when you're giving presentations?

1 Don't rely on technology.

_____

_____

2 Make it visual.

_____

_____

3 Get it right.

_____

_____

4 Less is more.

_____

_____

4 Read this extract from an article on how to give presentations. Circle the correct options.

Rehearsing your presentation

- It's a good idea to practise your presentation in front of friends and family. Ask them questions such as:

  Could you [1] *follow / followed* my presentation?

  Did you think I was [2] *knowledge / knowledgeable* about my subject?

  Was I speaking [3] *clear / clearly*? Could you hear me?

- If you're using slides or other visual material, include them in your rehearsal and practise the transition between slides or stages of your talk. Ask your practice audience questions such as:

  Were the pictures [4] *clear / clearly*?

  Were there [5] *too much / too many* pictures?

  Should there have been [6] *less / fewer* pictures?

  Were the transitions between one slide and the next [7] *smooth / smoothly*?

- Remember to time your presentation. If it's too long your audience will be [8] *bored / boring*.

Giving your presentation

- Spend a little time at the beginning [9] *make / making* your audience feel comfortable:

  'Welcome everyone. Thank you for coming.'

  'Can you hear me at the back of the room?'

- Make it clear whether you'd like people to [10] *interrupt / interrupting* with questions or to wait until the end:

  'There will be time at the end of the talk for any questions you may have.'

- You'll appear more confident if you [11] *look at / see* the audience, but don't just focus on one or two people. Make sure you include everyone.

- Use gestures and move around if it helps to [12] *illustrate / illustration* what you're saying.

- Don't hurry. You're more likely to speak too [13] *quick / quickly* than too [14] *slow / slowly*.

Getting your message across

1 This is the first part of a speech given by a headmistress at the end of term. Every seventh word is missing. Write a suitable word in each gap.

- Some may be simple words like *the* or *and*.
- Contractions, such as *didn't* (= *did not*), count as one word.
- There can be several possibilities for some of the gaps.

"Good afternoon, everyone. Now, I'm not [1] _____ to make a long speech, but [2] _____ just want to say a few [3] _____ about what we've all been doing [4] _____ the last year.

I'd like to [5] _____ by congratulating you all on doing [6] _____ well academically. The exam results are [7] _____ best we've ever had and I [8] _____ you've all worked really hard to [9] _____ them. Progress has been particularly good [10] _____ Maths, English and Science, which is [11] _____ encouraging.

Moving on now to other [12] _____ of the curriculum, like music, drama [13] _____ sport, we had a wonderful concert [14] _____ the end of the autumn term, [15] _____ by the school orchestra. And this [16] _____ we also had an evening when [17] _____ school jazz band performed for students [18] _____ their families. It was a huge [19] _____ and thoroughly enjoyed by everybody. We've [20] _____ just had the end-of-year [21] _____, which was written by our drama [22] _____, Mrs Atkins. Again, another big success.

[23] _____ the inter-schools sports event, we [24] _____ get first place but we did [25] _____ and we won two silver medals [26] _____ swimming. So again, well done to [27] _____ athletes and swimmers."

2 Read the second part of the headmistress's speech.

"Next, I'd like to talk about our links with the local community. It's been a great pleasure to see how many of you have taken part in community events. It shows that you care about other people. A good example of this is the 5-kilometre charity fun run around the park that many of you took part in to help buy computer equipment for schools in Africa.

And finally, I'd like to tell you about an exciting plan for the future. We will have a new drama studio by the middle of next year. At the moment, as you know, we've only got the school hall, in which you're now sitting, for our drama work and it's not always available, so we want a separate space which is just for drama.

To sum up, all of us are very pleased with what we've achieved this year, and we look forward to next year.

Have a happy holiday and thank you again for all your hard work."

Link these words and phrases from the text with the correct definitions.

1	links	**a**	a feeling of happiness or enjoyment
2	community	**b**	able to be used
3	pleasure	**c**	connections
4	charity	**d**	feel pleased and excited about something that's going to happen
5	available	**e**	independent, (*here*) not used for anything else
6	separate	**f**	raising money for a good cause
7	achieved	**g**	succeeded in doing
8	looked forward to	**h**	the people living in a particular area

3 **Read the conversation and report it.**

Mr Smith: Thank you Mrs Lewis. It was a very informative speech.

Mrs Lewis: Well, I like to keep parents informed about what is going on.

Mr Smith: And I think the new drama studio is a very good idea.

Mrs Lewis: Thank you.

Mr Lewis: Now, the school will need equipment for the new studio and I'd like to help with the lighting. My company specialises in stage lighting.

Mrs Lewis: I've been thinking about ways of raising money for the equipment. Perhaps you could come to our next school governors' meeting.

> **Language tip**
>
> When reporting a speech or a conversation, you can avoid repetition of 'said' by using verbs such as:
>
> add   remark
> answer   reply
> comment   respond
> exclaim   suggest
> offer

1 Mr Smith thanked Mrs Lewis and said that *it had been a very informative speech.*

2 Mrs Lewis replied that _____

_____

3 Mr Smith said that _____

4 He added that _____

and he offered to help with the lighting.

5 He said that _____

6 Mrs Lewis said that _____

and she suggested that he could come to the next school governors' meeting.

From ideas into words

1 Read Alicia's talk about her hometown. Which of the following does she do? Write 'yes' or 'no'.

	yes / no
1 She welcomes the audience.	
2 She gives an outline of what she's going to say.	
3 She makes it clear that she's starting the first section.	
4 She shows that she's starting a new section of the talk.	
5 She gives examples.	
6 She addresses the audience directly.	

I'm going to tell you about my hometown, Banyoles. I'm going to divide my talk into four parts. First, I'm going to talk about where the town is. Then I'm going to describe its main features. Next, I'll talk about special events in Banyoles. And finally, I'll tell you why it's a very good place to live.

First of all, where is Banyoles? It's in Catalonia, in the north-east of Spain. It's a medium-sized town with a population of 20,000. It is surrounded by hills and forests and you can see the snow-capped peaks of the Pyrenees to the northwest. By car, it's only an hour from Barcelona and it's half an hour from the beaches of the Costa Brava.

Moving on now to the main features of Banyoles, the focus of life here is definitely the lake. It's a pleasant place where people go to walk and to meet friends. It became world-famous when it was used for the rowing events in the Barcelona Olympic Games. It has become a centre for sports events such as swimming, rowing and canoeing. Twice a year there are swimming events in which local and international athletes swim the length of the lake: 2.1 kilometres.

A short walk from the lake takes you to the old town, with its medieval streets that lead to a central square, the Plaza Mayor. There is a weekly market that has been held in Banyoles since the 11th century. There are also museums, restaurants, cafés and shops.

There are several festivals throughout the year. One of the most attractive is the Exhibition of Flowers in June when many of the streets are decorated with colourful plants and flowers. However, the most important festival takes place for a week in October and includes a variety of cultural events, sports competitions and traditional contests such as the *castillers*, in which teams compete to build human towers. You might ask, what is a human tower? Well, it's a tower of people, standing on each other's shoulders!

Banyoles is a great place to live. It's a small, friendly town with plenty of sunshine and good weather for most of the year. A big advantage is that you can cycle everywhere and there are excellent sports facilities – a tennis club, a football club and a swimming club with outdoor swimming in the lake and an indoor heated pool. What more could you want?

2 Give Alicia advice on what she should put on the slides for her presentation. Write the key points for the slides and give ideas for pictures.

1

Banyoles

My hometown

Photo showing the lake at Banyoles

2

3

4

5

6

Learning and training

Good teachers, good learners

1 Match the items in the two columns to make complete phrases.

a good sense	model
a role	a difference
follow	of humour
in good	orders
low	self-esteem
make	shape

1 _____

2 _____

3 _____

4 _____

5 _____

6 _____

2 Use the phrases from Exercise 1 to complete what these people are saying about their jobs.

The great thing about being a fitness instructor is that you can

1 _____ to the way people feel about themselves. I've sometimes worked with clients who aren't

2 _____ and have 3 _____.

It's amazing the difference that working with them – just for a few weeks – can make.

In my job as an army instructor, communication and discipline are very important. You need to make people see it's important to

4 _____.

You need to be a leader rather than a follower because people look up to you as

5 _____.

To be a tour guide, you need to be outgoing and friendly and you need to have

6 _____.

And of course, it's helpful if you have a good loud speaking voice!

3 Complete what these people are saying about their jobs. Every seventh word is missing. Write a suitable word in each gap.

- Some may be simple words like *an* or *my*.
- There can be several possibilities for some of the gaps.

1 One of the nicest things about ^{1}_____ job is that you meet all
^{2}_____ of people from lots of different ^{3}_____ in the world.
That's why it's ^{4}_____ advantage if you can speak one ^{5}_____
more foreign languages. You need to ^{6}_____ a good communicator and make sure
^{7}_____ you're saying is interesting.

2 In this job you need to ^{1}_____ well-organised and enthusiastic. You need to
^{2}_____ good at multi-tasking - good at doing ^{3}_____ things at
once. You also need ^{4}_____ be quite creative and good at ^{5}_____
things. And above all, you need ^{6}_____ be very patient.

4 Write a sentence about a job that would suit you. Give your reasons using words and phrases from Exercises 2 and 3.

I think I would be a good primary school teacher because I'm quite creative ...

_____

_____

_____

_____

_____

_____

_____

5 Link the two halves of the sentences.

1 I'd like to be a writer because I'm good at making

2 My mum's a classroom assistant. She helps the children who fall

3 To be a good teacher, you have to be good at putting

4 My brother's brilliant with computers. If there's a problem, he can always work

5 You have to be good at getting people to join

6 It's hard being a junior doctor because you have to do

a across your ideas.

b in activities when you're a summer camp leader.

c out how to solve it.

d up stories.

e without sleep if there's an emergency.

f behind with their work.

Team spirit

1 Look at the poster and write the correct caption under each picture.

Abseiling (wearing a harness and a helmet)　　Dress wounds

Build a raft　　Make splints

Build a shelter　　Navigation by day and by night

Crawl through pipes　　Wade through mud

2 Decide which day of the course each of the following sentences refers to.

1　If you're staying overnight in an area where there are trees, you can do this.　___Day 1___

2　It's important to know what to do if there's an emergency and someone is injured.　_____

3　It's not just your feet that are going to get dirty. You'll be muddy from head to toe.　_____

4　This is important because tonight we'll be doing a night hike.　_____

5　You'll build your own form of transport, and then you'll use it.　_____

6　You'll learn how to come down a rock face from the top to the bottom.　_____

3 Write the words for these definitions. (They're on the poster that you have completed.)

1　A place made from branches and leaves where you can sleep. _____

2　Basic help that you give to a person who is ill or injured. _____

3　Finding the right direction to travel by using a map and other equipment. _____

4　A set of strong bands used for holding someone in a position or to stop them from falling.

_____

5　A flat piece of wood or metal used to keep a broken bone in position to help it mend.

_____

6　Make it from pieces of wood and use it to cross a river. _____

7　Walk through water that is not deep. _____

8　Move along on your hands and knees. _____

4 Correct these sentences.

1　These two <u>informations</u> are important. _____*These two pieces of information are important.*_____

2　A headtorch is a useful <u>equipment</u>. _____

3　I'll give you two important <u>advices</u>. _____

4　A waterproof jacket is an essential <u>clothing</u>. _____

A WEEKEND SURVIVAL COURSE

Are you ready for an adventure?

Day 1

Learn basic first-aid skills. You never know when you might need them.

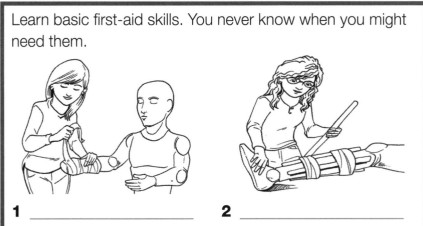

1 _____

2 _____

3 _____

Well it might not be home but it will keep you warm and dry!

Day 2

4 _____

_____

This is a good way of overcoming your fear of heights!

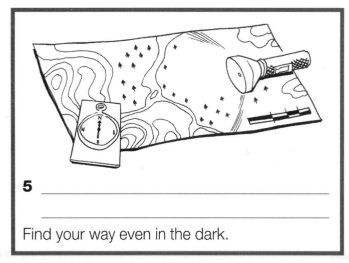

5 _____

_____

Find your way even in the dark.

Day 3

6 _____

You never know when you'll need to cross a river!

And then to finish, you just need to do the obstacle course.

7 _____

_____

8 _____

_____

What have you been doing?

1 Read the article and answer these questions.

1 What is KidZania?

_____

2 How big is it?

_____

3 Where is it?

_____

4 Who can go there?

_____

5 What's different about it?

_____

6 Who has put money into the project?

_____

7 Can you go to see a play there?

_____

8 How long can you stay there?

_____

9 How do the children's parents know where they are?

_____

10 What can adults do at KidZania?

_____

2 Find the words in the text for the following.

1 Money used in a particular country or place. _____

2 Amusement park rides with steep slopes and curves. _____

3 A room in a hospital where operations are done. _____

4 The place in a plane where the pilots sit. _____

5 The place in an airport where you find departures and arrivals. _____

6 Well-known companies or products. _____

7 Paid for (usually by a company which wants to advertise). _____

8 A period of time that is allowed for a particular activity. _____

Pit stop at KidZania

This is KidZania, a new mini-city built in London, where children are in charge. It has its own airport, hospital, police station, restaurants, shops, vehicles and currency.

The 7000 square metre attraction at Westfield, a shopping centre in west London, gives children aged four to 14 free rein to live like an adult and try out real-life professions.

Children service a racing car at KidZania in Westfield London, Shepherd's Bush

Ollie Vigors, director of KidZania, said the experience was "entertaining and educational and not necessarily in that order".

Instead of having rollercoasters and other rides like a traditional theme park, KidZania recreates adult workplaces such as an operating theatre, a plane cockpit, a TV studio and a bank, all at two-thirds lifesize. Children arrive at KidZania through a British Airways-branded terminal and an 18-metre A319 aircraft.

Other brands such as H&M, Gourmet Burger Kitchen, Renault and Dorsett Hotels have sponsored the city's 45 shops and other businesses, where children take part in staffed activities and earn "money" called KidZos. They can then spend their KidZos in KidZania's mini shopping mall or on activities such as the theatre. During their four-hour slot, which is monitored via a digital wristband for safety, youngsters can go anywhere in the city, which is said to have cost £20 million to build.

Adults can enter but are not allowed to take part in the activity with their children.

The ideal job

1 Solve the crossword.

Across

Someone who ...

5 writes articles for a newspaper. (10)

7 paints pictures. (6)

13 repairs cars. (8)

14 (See 2 Down.)

15 is a member of the army. (7)

16 looks after animals when they are ill. (3)

17 (See 9 Down.)

Down

Someone who ...

1 (With 12 Down.) designs clothes. (7, 8)

2 (With 14 Across.) plans and builds roads, bridges and large buildings. (5, 8)

3 looks after people when they are ill or injured. (6)

4 composes and plays music. (8)

6 cuts and styles hair. (11)

8 may be a chemist, a physicist or a biologist. (9)

9 (With 17 Across.) catches criminals and protects people and property. (6, 7)

10 organises a business and is responsible for its activities. (7)

11 teaches at a university. (8)

12 (See 1 Down.)

2 Each of these people is talking about an advantage of their job. Describe each advantage (make a 'collocation') using a word from each box.

job	hours
flexible	employment
good	work
regular	satisfaction
seasonal	prospects

> I like my job as a graphic designer because I can choose when I start and finish – within limits, of course.

1 _____

> I work in a holiday resort, which suits me, because I only work in the summer months. It means I have time to study during the rest of the year.

2 _____

> I don't earn a lot of money doing gardening work but I love working outside so I really enjoy it.

3 _____

> I'm lucky because, as an IT consultant, I always have work.

4 _____

> At the moment I'm doing quite a lot of basic jobs in the office but it's worth it because the opportunities for doing more interesting work and for earning more money are very good.

5 _____

3 Find a sentence in Box B which could follow a sentence in Box A. Join the sentences using one of these phrases: (Remember to use a comma before *which*.)

which I like because   which is good because

which I wouldn't like because   which means that

A

My mum works for an international company.

My dad is self-employed.

I help my aunt and uncle in their shop on a Saturday.

If my mum gets a new job, we might have to go to live in another country.

B

I would miss my friends.

He's usually at home when I get home from school.

I earn a bit of pocket money.

She's often away from home.

1 _____

_____

2 _____

_____

3 _____

_____

4 _____

_____

Part-time and summer jobs

1 It's a good idea to try to predict the questions you might be asked at an interview. Write one question an interviewer might ask somebody applying for a part-time job at each of the following:

1 a riding stables

_____

2 a farm

_____

3 a garden centre

_____

4 a hotel

_____

5 an office

_____

2 Choose two of the questions you've written in Exercise 1. How would a good candidate answer them?

_____

_____

_____

_____

_____

3 In your notebook, write an email for a part-time job. Follow the example but give your own details.

- Choose a part-time job that would suit you.
- Say why you would be good for the job.

> Dear Sir / Madam
>
> I am writing to apply for a part-time job at Go-Kart Fun.
>
> I am 13 years old and I will be 14 next month. I'm enthusiastic about karting. I'm a good communicator and I'm very patient – I've got three younger brothers and sisters.
>
> I go to Westway Secondary School. I speak English and I also speak a little French and Spanish.
>
> I would like to work on Saturday or Sunday afternoons. I would be happy to come for an interview after school one day.
>
> I look forward to hearing from you.
>
> Yours faithfully
>
> Daniel Palmer

4 Complete the chart with the reflexive pronouns.

subject pronoun	object pronoun	possessive adjective	reflexive pronoun
I	me	my	*myself*
you (*singular*)	you	your	
he	him	his	
she	her	her	
it	it	its	
we	us	our	
you (*plural*)	you	your	
they	them	their	

5 Read the conversation and write in the correct reflexive pronouns.

Dad: You did well to get [1] ____*yourself*____ a part-time job at the karting track. How was your first day?

Daniel: It was absolutely brilliant. I really enjoyed [2] _____. I helped at a children's party. There were twenty children there, all about seven years old.

Dad: Did they behave [3] _____?

Daniel: Well, sort of. They were very noisy. You couldn't hear [4] _____ speak. They just wanted to get into the karts. One little boy ran so fast to get into the first car that he fell over.

Dad: Did he hurt [5] _____?

Daniel: No, he was fine. When they'd finished the karting, they all had sandwiches and a drink.

Dad: How did that go?

Daniel: Well, it was a bit messy.

Dad: Did you have anything to eat?

Daniel: Yes, we helped [6] _____ to what was left.

Go-Kart Fun

Young entrepreneurs

1 What do you call these people? The words in bold give you a clue.

Someone who ...

1 **participates** in a sport or another activity is a _____participant_____.

2 enters a **contest** is a _____

3 you **consult** about computers is an IT _____

4 helps you with your finances and does your **accounts** is an _____

5 **invents** things is an _____

6 **instructs** you about how to drive a car is a driving _____

7 **acts** on the stage is an _____

8 **lectures** at a university is a _____

9 **fights** fires is a _____

10 **designs** graphics is a graphic _____

11 **presents** TV programmes is a TV _____

12 writes for a **journal** is a _____

13 gives beauty **therapy** is a beauty _____

14 works in a **pharmacy** is a _____

15 works in an office or hotel **reception** is a _____

> **Study skills**
>
> It's a good idea, when recording vocabulary, to include words which are connected grammatically, e.g.
> verb: participate
> noun (person): participant
> noun (activity): participation
>
> verb: design
> noun (person): designer
> noun (activity): design

2 Look at the picture of the TV studio, where last-minute preparations for *Junior Chef of the Year* are being made. Use a noun from Box A and a verb from Box B to describe what is happening.

A

The presenter	The ingredients
The floor	The water jug
The microphones	The presenter's script
One of the ovens	The programme title

B

clean	prepare
correct	repair
fill	test
make up	type

1 The presenter is being made up.
2 The water jug is being filled.
3
4
5
6
7
8
9
10

13 Population and resources

People and places

1 Link the two halves of each sentence.

1 The first thing you notice about Brazil
2 Sixty-two per cent of Brazilians are under 30, which is one of the reasons
3 The climate in the south-east
4 The south-east is warm in summer
5 The major cities, São Paulo and Rio de Janeiro,
6 São Paulo is a financial and industrial centre,
7 Rio de Janeiro is a tourist destination with
8 There are good communication links between Rio de Janeiro and other cities and countries by road,

a and it doesn't get too cold in winter.
b are densely populated.
c by sea and by air.
d great beaches and a world-famous carnival.
e is that it's a country of young people.
f makes it a comfortable place to live.
g providing jobs for workers from other parts of Brazil.
h that there's such a feeling of energy and enthusiasm.

2 Answer these questions about Brazil. The information is in Exercise 1.

1 Where would you go to look for work?

2 Which city is a good place to go on holiday and why?

3 Which is the best area to live and why?

4 Why does Brazil have a feeling of energy and enthusiasm?

5 Can you go by ship and by plane to Rio de Janeiro?

3 Complete the text about Brazil with words from the list.

climate	crops	exporter	production	sparsely
commodity	dense	populated	settlement	textile

Outside the major cities, the south-east is moderately [1] _____. It is the country's main agricultural area, due to its temperate [2] _____ and fertile soil, making it ideal for cattle farming and for growing a variety of [3] _____. Brazil is the world's largest producer and [4] _____ of sugar, coffee and orange juice.

The Amazon Basin, a vast area spreading across the north of the country, has an extremely hot, wet climate. Its [5] _____ tropical rainforest makes communication difficult and the poor soil is not good for farming. It is the most [6] _____ populated area of Brazil. However, there is one exception and that is Manaus, which, in the 19th century, grew from a small [7] _____ into a major city. This was due to the [8] _____ of rubber from rubber trees, which were only found in the Amazon Basin. Rubber was a valuable [9] _____. It had many uses, such as in steam engines and other machines, in the [10] _____ industry for waterproofing, and, of course, eventually for tyres for bicycles and cars.

4 Rewrite these sentences using the words in brackets.

1 By 2015, the population of Switzerland had risen to 8 million.
(Use *increase*) _____
_____

2 In Indonesia in 2015, 5% of the population was over 5 and under 9 years old.
(Use *between*) _____
_____

3 In Greece, the number of people working in agriculture decreased from 1.4 million in 2000 to 1.2 million in 2010.
(Use *fall*) _____
_____

4 The population of Detroit in the USA rose to 1.86 million in 1950 and had fallen to 700,000 by 2012.
(Use *increase, decrease*) _____
_____

Japan: A case study

1 Make compound nouns from the words in the two circles to match these definitions.

1 People within a certain age range.

_____

2 How long people are likely to live.

_____

3 The number of babies born during a period of time in a particular place.

_____

4 The number of people who die during a period of time in a particular place.

_____

5 Someone who is paid to look after other people.

_____

6 A detailed report containing information which illustrates general principles.

_____

death
age   case
care   birth
life

worker
rate   study
expectancy
rate
group

Your written work will be more interesting if you vary the way you express your ideas.

For example, the verbs *fall*, *decrease* and *go down* have a similar meaning when you're writing about numbers and quantities. You can also use the nouns *a fall, a decrease, a decline*. Rather than repeating the same word, choose a synonym (a word that means the same thing).

2 Complete the sentences.

By 2050 ...

1 life expectancy (*rise*) _will have risen_ .

2 life expectancy (*increase*)

_____

3 life expectancy (*go up*)

_____

4 there (*be / an increase*)

_____ in life expectancy.

What can you say about the meaning of these four sentences?

_____

3 Write a sentence about what will have happened to the populations of each of the following countries between now and 2100. Remember to vary the words you use to describe the changes.

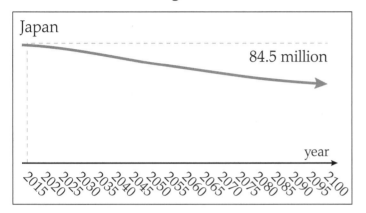

1 Between now and 2100, the population of Japan _____

_____

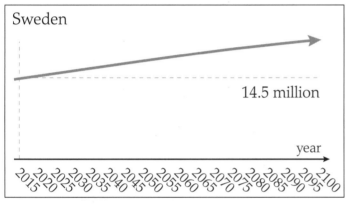

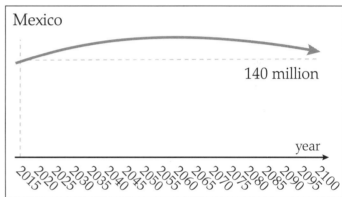

2 _____

_____

_____

3 _____

_____

_____

4 Answer the questions giving your own opinions.

1 If the birth rate in a particular country or area is going to increase significantly in the next ten years, what does this mean for schools?

Schools will need more … _____

_____

_____

2 If the population of a country is predicted to rise significantly, what does this mean for towns and cities?

There will need to be more … _____

_____

_____

Water for the world

1 Solve the crossword.

Across

1 Earth, for example, or Venus or Mars. (6)

4 To calculate the approximate amount or size of something. (8)

6 Relating to the whole world. (6)

7 Say what you think will happen in the future. (7)

10 Desalination is the process of turning salt water into _____ water. (5)

12 Belonging or relating to the home. (8)

15 The production of goods in factories, for example, the textile _____ . (8)

16 Important and necessary. (9)

17 Water, oil, wood and coal are all natural _____ . (9)

18 Cloth or material for making clothes. (6)

Down

2 Having the same value. (10)

3 A material from which T-shirts are often made. (6)

5 The practice or science of farming. (11)

8 Now, at the present time. (9)

9 A company that makes things in large quantities. (12)

11 Not endless, the opposite of *infinite*. (6)

13 People who buy and use products and services. (9)

14 1,000,000,000 – a thousand million. (7)

2 Read the text and circle the correct options. Then put the percentages in the correct places on the diagram.

[1]*Although / Either* we think of rivers, lakes and reservoirs as being the major sources of fresh water for the planet, in fact, they only provide 0.5% of the earth's fresh water. Thirty per cent of the world's fresh water is to be found underground and surprisingly, 69.5% is in the form of glaciers.

Both agriculture and industry use a lot of water. Industry uses 22% [2]*both / whereas* agriculture uses more than three times that amount.

Only 1% of the water we use at home is for drinking while 6% is used for preparing food. If we want to save water at home, we could cut down on the amount we use [3]*or / either* for household cleaning(34%) [4]*or / either* in the bathroom (59%), or indeed, both.

We can survive [5]*although / provided that* we don't waste the water we have. We need to focus [6]*both / and* on recycling more water [7]*both / and* on new methods of obtaining fresh water, for example through desalination.

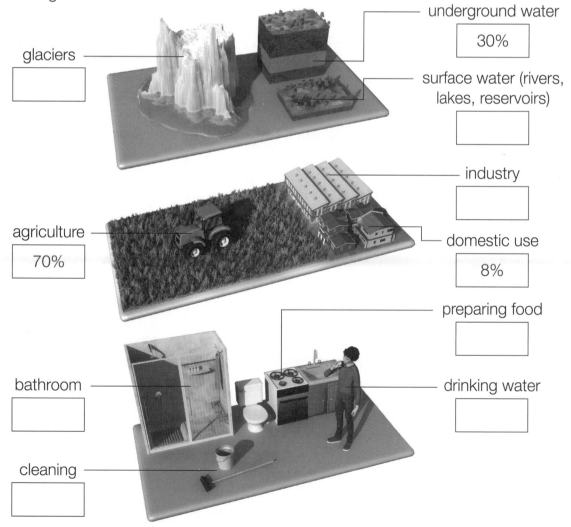

glaciers [ ]

underground water [30%]

surface water (rivers, lakes, reservoirs) [ ]

industry [ ]

agriculture [70%]

domestic use [8%]

preparing food [ ]

bathroom [ ]

drinking water [ ]

cleaning [ ]

14 Cultures and customs

What's in a name?

1 Rewrite the two sentences as one using a past participle clause, as in the example.

1 Several names have been invented by writers. They include Miranda in Shakespeare's play *The Tempest* and Wendy in J.M. Barrie's play *Peter Pan*.

Names invented by writers include Miranda in Shakespeare's play The Tempest and Wendy in

J.M. Barrie's play Peter Pan.

2 A dessert was created in honour of the famous Russian ballerina, Anna Pavlova. It is called 'a pavlova'.

The dessert

3 Middle names are used to keep family traditions alive. They are sometimes quite unusual.

Middle names

4 A type of breathable, waterproof fabric is called Gore-tex. It is named after Wilbert L Gore and Robert Gore.

The breathable, waterproof fabric

5 In the 18th century, images were cut out of paper or black card. They were known as silhouettes, after Etienne de Silhouette.

In the 18th century, images

6 Several well-known nineteenth-century novels were written by women. Many of them were published under pen-names.

Many well-known nineteenth-century novels

2 Read the text and write the examples in the correct places.

Examples
- Cook, Baker, Butcher
- Adam, which means 'red skin' and Valerie which means 'strong'
- Elizabeth Jane Weston and James Francis Edward Stuart
- April (born in April) and Francis (from France)
- Felix, which means 'happy' and Amy, which means 'loved'
- Hill, Field, Wood
- John F. Kennedy
- Johnson (John's son)
- Little, Rich, Young, Fox

Personal names in English are generally classified into three types: the first name (or given name), the middle name and the surname (or family name). In the early Middle Ages (from the 5th to 10th century), there were only first names. Surnames came later. They were additional names used to identify people who had the same given name. The word surname comes from the French *sur + nom*. It is found in English from the 14th century.

First names

First names were sometimes chosen to describe a physical characteristic. Examples: (1)

_____

_____

_____

They can also describe parents' feelings. Examples: (2)

_____

_____

_____

First names can also reflect the time of birth or place of origin. Examples: (3)

_____

_____

_____

Middle names

In the 17th century, people started using one or more middle names. Examples: (4)

_____

_____

_____

The American fashion was often to refer to the middle name simply by an initial letter. This tradition continues today. Example: (5)

_____

Surnames

Some surnames come from a place name or describe a geographical feature, showing where a person came from. Examples: (6)

_____

Others show what job a person did. Examples: (7)

_____

Another group shows family relationships. Example: (8)

_____

Finally, there are surnames which came from nicknames, expressing a physical or other identifying feature. Examples: (9)

_____

Ceremonies and special occasions

1 Put these words and phrases in the correct column in the chart.

get engaged	celebrate	get married	marriage	celebration
invite	engagement	invitation	propose	proposal

verb / verb phrase	Noun
get engaged	engagement

2 Choose from the words and phrases in Exercise 1 to complete this dialogue.

A: We had a big family ¹_____ last weekend.

B: Why was that? What were you celebrating?

A: Well, it was an ²_____ party for my sister and Matthew, my brother-in-law to be.

B: Wow! I didn't know she was going to get engaged.

A: I know, it was very exciting. First, Matthew asked my dad if he could ³_____ to my sister.

B: What did your dad say?

A: Well, he said yes of course. So Matthew and my sister went out to dinner and he asked her to be his wife!

B: And did she accept his ⁴_____ immediately?

A: Yes, she did.

B: When are they going to ⁵_____? Have they set the date for the wedding yet?

A: Yes, they have. They're just deciding who they're going to ⁶_____ and then they'll send out the ⁷_____.

Language tip

A *wedding* is the ceremony and the celebration which take place when a couple gets married. *What's the date of the wedding?* NOT ~~What's the date of the marriage?~~

Marriage is the relationship between husband and wife. *My grandparents were married for fifty years. They had a very happy marriage.*

Say: *She married him* or *She got married to him.* NOT ~~She got married with him.~~

3 Solve the crossword.

Across

3 A present, something that is given. (4)

4 A woman who is getting married. (5)

6 A band, usually made of precious metal, worn on a finger. (4)

7 A man who is getting married. (5)

10 The time when you are an adult. (9)

11 A social event at which people meet to celebrate something. (5)

12 A belief or way of doing something that has existed for a long time. (9)

Down

1 The time when you are a child. (9)

2 Someone who lives near you. (9)

5 A formal event with special words and actions, such as a wedding. (8)

8 A circle made of flowers and leaves. (7)

9 A short well-known statement that gives practical advice about life. (7)

4 Use these prompts to write about engagements and weddings in Pakistan. Use the present passive.

To mark an engagement ...

a special ceremony / hold

garlands of flowers / give

rings / exchanged

a date for the wedding / set

close friends and family / invite

a special ceremony is held.

_____

_____

_____

_____

_____

_____

At the wedding ...

wedding tents / put up

brightly coloured traditional costumes / wear

the marriage contract / sign

a special dinner / serve

_____

_____

_____

_____

_____

_____

Pearls of wisdom

1 Link the two halves of each proverb.

1	Don't put all your eggs	**a**	are free.
2	Early to bed and early to rise	**b**	by its cover.
3	Every cloud has a	**c**	is worth two in the bush.
4	Better safe	**d**	don't make a right.
5	Many hands make	**e**	light work.
6	Never judge a book	**f**	makes a man healthy, wealthy and wise.
7	The best things in life	**g**	the other side of the fence.
8	The grass is always greener on	**h**	in one basket.
9	Two wrongs	**i**	than sorry.
10	A bird in the hand	**j**	silver lining.

2 Write the proverb from Exercise 1 which matches each of the following meanings.

1 _____

If someone does something bad to you, it doesn't help to do something bad in return.

2 _____

It always seems as though other people are more fortunate than you.

3 _____

It's a good idea to spread your risk, so don't depend on just one thing for success.

4 _____

Something that you definitely have is better than several uncertain possibilities.

5 _____

You can find something good even in the worst situations.

3 Write out the remaining proverbs from Exercise 1 and write what they mean.

1 Proverb: _____

  Meaning: _____

2 Proverb: _____

  Meaning: _____

3 Proverb: _____

  Meaning: _____

4 Proverb: _____

  Meaning: _____

5 Proverb: _____

  Meaning: _____

4 Which of the proverbs in Exercise 1 …

1 rhymes?

_____

2 features alliteration (words beginning with the same sounds)?

_____

3 means the opposite of 'Too many cooks spoil the broth'?

_____

4 is metaphorical (uses one idea to express another)? Give two examples.

_____

_____

5 Complete the conversations with an appropriate proverb from Exercise 1.

1

Sonia: We've got a new girl in our class. She doesn't talk to anyone. She looks
           really unfriendly.

Zainab: Oh I know the girl you mean. She lives near me so I've met her at the bus
           stop. She's quite shy but she's really nice when you talk to her.

Sonia: Really?

Zainab: Yes, she is, and you know what they say: _____

2

Dad: Are you going out to play football again? What about your homework?

Selim: Oh, I'll do that later. I just want to concentrate on football. You have to play
           as much as you can if you want to be a professional footballer.

Dad: Selim, I know that's your dream but you've got to be realistic. Only a few
           people make it as professional players. You need to do well in your school
           exams so that you've got a choice of career. You know what they say:

_____

3

Aida: I was so sorry to hear you broke your leg. It must have been awful. Did you
           get bored being at home all the time?

Lucy: It was a bit boring at first, but then I thought, I've always wanted to learn
           the guitar and now I've got time to do it. So I spent some money I'd saved
           on a guitar and a teach-yourself app. I love it and I'm going to have lessons.
           As they say: _____

6 In your notebook, write a conversation, like the ones in Exercise 5,
   which ends in a proverb.

Zoom in!

1 Read the clues and write the answers.

Quiz

1 It's useful to have this book when you're learning a language.
a dictionary

2 Some people write about what's happened during the day. Others use it to remind them about appointments.
_____

3 It's got days, dates and months. It lasts a year and you can put it up on the wall.
_____

4 It's an educational book that you use in your lessons at school.
_____

5 It's old-fashioned and you have to fill it with ink. But you can write really well with it. _____

6 It's sometimes called a ballpoint pen. You can write in blue, black, red or green. It's usually made of plastic and it's quite cheap. _____

7 You can write or draw with it. If you make a mistake, you can rub it out and start again. _____

8 You can download books onto this digital device. _____

9 Some people said that digital books would replace these but it hasn't happened. _____

10 These are very useful when you want to look up facts and information. Examples include encyclopedias and atlases.
_____

2 Identify these objects.

a

b

c

_____   _____   _____

3 Circle the correct options.

1 I've just sent you an email but I forgot to *add / attach* the document you needed. Sorry! Here it is.

2 I lost a whole morning's work when my computer *crashed / fell down*.

3 When I try to open a new web page, the screen just *freezes / sticks*.

4 To do a screen grab, hold down the shift key and the command key and *push / press* 4.

5 Can you read this *in screen / on screen* or do you want me to print it out for you?

4 Complete the conversation with the correct verb + preposition / particle. Remember to use the correct form of the verb.

IT support: Hello, IT Support, how can I help you?

Client: I've got a problem with my laptop. Every time I try to
¹ _____ a document _____ an email, the screen freezes.

IT support: Right. Have you ² _____ _____ your hard disk recently?

Client: Yes, it does it automatically. It backs up every few minutes.

IT support: Good, and can you switch the machine off?

Client: No, I can't, as I say the screen's frozen.

IT support: Oh yes. OK. Well, ³ _____ _____ the on / off button for
five seconds. That will ⁴ _____ the machine _____.

Client: OK, I'll do that now. Right.

IT support: Then wait a few minutes. ⁵ _____ the computer _____
again and try sending an email with an attachment. If you still have
problems, bring it in and we'll see what we can do.

switch
back
switch
attach
hold

off
down
on
to
up

5 Now complete this conversation in the same way.

Receptionist: Hello, Roundwood Park Sports Centre. How can I help you?

Customer: Hello. Yes, I want to download the application form for becoming a lifeguard at the
pool, but I can't work out how to do it.

Receptionist: Are you at your computer now?

Customer: Yes.

Receptionist: And have you ¹ _____ _____ to the sports centre website?

Customer: Yes. I've logged in and I've ² _____ _____ my password
but I can't find the link to the application form.

Receptionist: Right. You need to ³ _____ _____, right to the bottom of
the page.

Customer: OK. Oh yes, I can see it now.

Receptionist: ⁴ _____ _____ the link.

Customer: The print is quite small.

Receptionist: You can ⁵ _____ _____ on the details.

Customer: Oh yes, I can read it now.

Receptionist: You can either fill in the form online or you can ⁶ _____ it _____ and keep a copy.

click
print   log
type   scroll
zoom

in
down   in
on   out
in

That's a good idea!

1 Read the text. Explain briefly in writing why Lauren Bowker is an unusual fashion designer.

Art meets science

Lauren Bowker, who designs wearable technology, is interested not only in art and design, but also in chemistry.

When she was in her first year at university studying textiles, Lauren became extremely ill and spent several months in hospital. It was then that she decided that she wanted to design clothes with a purpose. So she went to the chemistry department of the university to study chemistry. She wanted to create a jacket which would absorb pollution. That was just the start.

Lauren saw an opportunity for a designer who understood science and could apply it creatively, bringing technology and art together. Chemistry provided the stimulation she needed to make her designs really different. Her inspiration comes from places like the Natural History Museum and from lectures in Astrophysics.

The place where Lauren works is part laboratory and part studio. Examples of her recent creations include a bag which changes colour when you touch it (and each person who touches it creates a different colour). She has also designed a pen with a feather top which changes colour in contact with the air. There's also a notebook which changes colour with the seasons and a scarf which changes colour in reaction to movement.

_____

_____

_____

2 Write the nouns that come from these verbs. They are all in the text.

verbs	nouns
pollute	
stimulate	
inspire	
create	
react	

3 Read the text again and tick (✔) the correct answer.

1 Lauren first went to university to study

    a chemistry

    b textiles

    c physics

2 Her aim, after starting to study chemistry, was to make clothes that reacted to

    a the environment

    b light

    c movement

3 Lauren gets a lot of her ideas from

    a science

    b history

    c art

4 Lauren designs

    a only clothes

    b electronic gadgets

    c clothes, accessories and writing materials

4 Which of the things that Lauren has created would you like to have and why?

_____

_____

5 Read the selling points for an item of clothing which uses technology. Circle the correct option in each sentence.

1 The new GPS performance monitoring vest has *even / just* more functions than the previous model.

2 It's becoming very popular, *simply / particularly* with football players and their coaches.

3 It's very comfortable and easy to wear. You *particularly / simply* wear it with a training top.

4 The athletes who use these devices are *just / mainly* football players.

5 It's *just / especially* useful for coaches and medical staff because it gives a detailed analysis of the players' movements.

6 It measures not *only / also* speed but *only / also* changes in direction.

7 It isn't *just / especially* a gadget.

8 It *particularly / even* has a wireless connection to a computer.

Language tip

Use focusing adverbs such as *especially, even* and *just* to add emphasis to what you are saying. This will help your writing to sound more interesting.

The future is digital

1 Read the extracts from an interview with an educational psychologist. Complete them with the words from the box.

apps	mobile phones	tablet	TV	website
interacting	MP3 players		video games	
Internet	screen	technology		websites

"We have to remember that children today are different from when we were young. My generation watched ¹_____. We were passive, we didn't interact with it. Children and teenagers today are very sophisticated. They've grown up with ²_____ so they don't have a problem using their mobile phones, listening to their ³_____ and playing ⁴_____. They switch from one to another very easily.

Young people today do seem able to divide their attention, between, let's say, homework and their ⁵_____. And think about it, with the ⁶_____ and with ⁷_____, they've got access to a lot of information, which is great when you're doing a research project, for example. And teachers say that students can become more independent learners.

It's very easy, as we all know, to take stuff directly from ⁸_____ and present it as your own, so it is a problem getting students to realise that that's not the way to learn. You need to engage with the information and you need to refer to more than one ⁹_____ to make sure you've got your facts right.

In our research we did find that parents were more likely to buy their 3- or 4-year-old a ¹⁰_____ than a teddy bear – which is a bit sad! This does mean that some children arrive at school at the age of 5 finding it quite hard to concentrate and even to mix with other children because they're so used to ¹¹_____ with a ¹²_____, which isn't good."

2 Put the adverbs in the correct places in the sentences.

extremely

1 It's ∧ easy to find your way around a new city with GPS on your phone. (*extremely*)

2 I find memory sticks are useful when I'm moving between one computer and another. (*quite*)

3 Connections to the internet are faster now than they used to be. (*a lot*)

4 I use a computer so much that I find it difficult to write with a pen now. (*rather*)

5 Watching a DVD on your laptop is a different experience from watching a film on a big cinema screen. (*totally*)

6 The new smartwatches are amazing. (*absolutely*)

7 This phone is as light as the old model but it's bigger. (*slightly*)

8 That new laptop is nice but it's expensive. (*very, too*)

> **Language tip**
>
> Be careful about using *very* and *too*.
> *Too* means 'more than enough', 'more than is right', or 'more than is necessary'.
>
> *It's too expensive.*
> = *It's more expensive than it should be.*
>
> *It's very expensive.*
> = *It costs a lot of money.*

3 Read the information about a new product. Then use the questions to write a paragraph in your notebook about it.

Product	A smart umbrella: 'The Sensing Umbrella'
Designers	Three students: Simon Herzog, Saurabh Datta and Akarsh Sanghi, alumni of the Copenhagen Institute of Interaction Design.
Function	Monitors / measures air pollution levels (carbon monoxide and nitrogen dioxide). LED lights on umbrella show pollution levels (change colour and rhythm). Data ⇒ pollution databases in the Cloud.
Aim	Create network of users ⇒ monitor air quality.

The Sensing Umbrella

- What is it called and what is it?
- Who designed it?
- What is it for and how does it work?

A trick of the light

1 Solve the crossword.

Across

5 The top layer of something. (7)

8 Seen for the first time on stage or at the cinema. (9)

10 To start to be seen or to suddenly be seen. (6)

12 A performance or series of performances of a play. (10)

13 The opposite of dark. (5)

15 Not able to be seen. (6)

16 90° is a right _____. (5)

17 The place where you go to see a play. (7)

18 Pepper's Ghost is an optical _____. (8)

Down

1 A piece of special glass in which you can see yourself. (6)

2 The opposite of *10 Across*. (9)

3 Actors perform on this. (5)

4 Another word for 'under'. (5)

5 A large flat piece, for example, of glass. (Also of linen and of paper.) (5)

6 Picture, often one you see in your mind. (5)

7 A hundred years. (7)

9 What you see when you look in *1 Down*. (10)

11 The people who watch a play. (8)

14 A three-dimensional image produced by lasers. (8)

17 A clever way of doing something, also something that you do to deceive someone. (5)

2 How might the following be used to create special effects in a theatre production?

1 a film projector

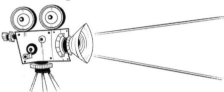

You can project an image or multiple images onto a sheet of white cloth or a screen at the back of the stage to give the impression of a landscape with mountains, for example. You could also project moving images to give the impression of, for example, a sea voyage or a crowd scene.

2 dry ice

3 a wind machine

4 a trapdoor (a hole) in the floor of the stage

How we see the world

1 Every seventh word in this article is missing.
Write a suitable word in each gap.

- Some may be simple words like *of* or *a*.
- Contractions, such as *couldn't* (= *could not*), count as one word.
- There can be more than one possibility for some of the gaps.

After buying a dress for her [1] _____ wedding, Cecilia Bleasdale sent
a photo [2] _____ it to her daughter, Grace. Grace [3] _____
understand why her mum had chosen [4] _____ light-coloured dress in
white and gold. [5] _____ her husband-to-be, Keir, said 'It's not
[6] _____ and gold. It's blue and black.' [7] _____ couldn't agree on
the colour so [8] _____ friend, Caitlin, posted the photo of [9] _____
dress on the Internet and the [10] _____ went viral. Within hours the dress
[11] _____ quickly became the top trending item [12] _____ Twitter
around the world.

We asked [13] _____ in the street what colour they [14] _____ the
dress was. Sixty-nine per cent [15] _____ it was white and gold. Thirty-one
[16] _____ cent said it was black and [17] _____ .

2 Write answers to these questions, giving your own ideas and opinions.

1 What do you associate with these colours? Think of the natural world, places, feelings, …

   a blue _____

   b red _____

   c green _____

   d yellow _____

2 If you were the manager of a football team, what colours would you choose for the club kit and why?

_____

_____

3 It's very rare to see food that is blue. Imagine that the food on your plate at your next meal was dyed blue, so you had blue rice, blue vegetables and even blue fish. What would your reaction be?

_____

_____

3 The phrases in the box explain the numbered phrases below.
Write them in the correct places.

- they can detect far more different shades of colour than other people because they have four colour receptors.

- they have only two colour receptors. Their eyes only detect blue and green.

- this helps them find food.

- they have three different colour receptors and can detect red, blue and green.

Language tip

The prefix *tri* comes from a Greek word meaning 'three'.

The prefix *tetra* comes from a Greek word meaning 'four'.

1 Most humans are trichromatic: _____

_____

2 Some people are colour blind: _____

_____

3 A few people are tetrachromatic: _____

_____

4 Birds are tetrachromatic: _____

4 Complete each sentence with the correct phrase from the box. Remember to put the verb in the *-ing* form after the conjunctions.

- after (*win*) the Pritzker Prize for architecture. She was the first woman to do so.
- before (*paint*) a picture.
- since (*make*) her film *Wadjda*, about a girl who dreams of having a bicycle.
- when (*take*) photographs during his first visit to Yosemite National Park, aged 14.

1 Most artists do a sketch _____

_____

2 The film director and writer, Haifaa al-Mansour, has become known around the world _____

_____

_____

3 The architect Zaha Hadid became world famous _____

_____

_____

4 Ansel Adams became interested in both photography and the environment _____

_____

_____

Sounds good to me!

1 Use the words from the box to write about what's happening in the picture.

Language tip

When you add –*ing* to a word ending in *e*, you usually drop the *e*:

sizzle → sizzling

The –*ing* form of *clip-clop* is *clip-clopping*.

A sunny day in the park

The children are shrieking with laughter.

_____

_____

_____

_____

_____

_____

_____

_____

_____

_____

buzz	a tune
clip-clop	along the path.
rustle	around the flowers.
shriek	each other in the water.
sizzle	in the pan.
splash	in the wind.
whistle	through the air.
whizz	with laughter.

2 Circle the correct option.

A wet day in town

What a miserable day! It was the last day before the holiday and everybody was [1] *crashing / dashing* about trying to get their shopping done. Some of the shoppers were [2] *grumbling / groaning* because the shopping centre hadn't opened on time. One of the men standing in the queue had a terrible cold. He was coughing and [3] *spluttering / crackling* and he looked awful. Someone had set the fire alarm off and it was [4] *clanging / tinkling* and making a terribly loud noise. It wasn't raining hard but it was [5] *sprinkling / drizzling* and water was slowly [6] *trickling / spitting* off the roof onto the people in the queue.

3 Find onomatopoeic words in Exercises 1 and 2 to add to these word groups.

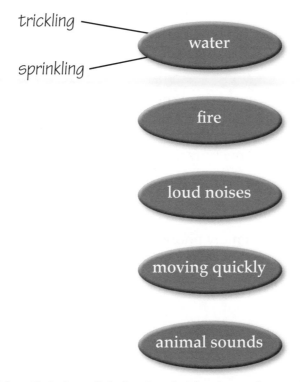

trickling

sprinkling

water

fire

loud noises

moving quickly

animal sounds

Right and wrong

Crime and punishment

1 Read what happened and complete the words for the crimes.

What happened?	What was the crime?
1 He took something from a shop without paying for it.	s h o p _ _ _ _ _ _ _ _
2 They got into the house by breaking a window and they stole jewellery and cash.	b u r g _ _ _ _ _
3 He took the purse from her bag and ran off with it.	t h _ _ _ _
4 They stole a car and drove around the town, before leaving it in a supermarket car park.	j o y _ _ _ _ _ _ _
5 They surrounded him and forced him to hand over his smartphone and his wallet.	m u g _ _ _ _ _
6 A gang went into the bank and told the cashiers to hand over all the cash.	r o b _ _ _ _ _
7 The police believe that the building was set on fire on purpose.	a r _ _ _ _

2 In this account of crime, every seventh word is missing.
Write a suitable word in each gap.

- Contractions, such as *didn't* (= *did not*), count as one word.
- There can be more than one possibility for some of the gaps.

I was walking through the shopping ⁱ _____ early on Saturday morning.
There weren't ² _____ people around and I was just ³ _____
in a shop window. Suddenly, there ⁴ _____ someone in front of me.
He ⁵ _____ me to hand over my mobile ⁶ _____.
I said 'No'. He grabbed my ⁷ _____, pulled me towards him, and said
⁸ '_____ me your phone or else'. I ⁹ _____ want to
get hurt so I ¹⁰ _____ him my phone.

3 Correct the 10 mistakes in Dave's account of a crime. Look for missing words and grammatical mistakes.

                      were

I was with some friends in a café and we ∧ chatting and laughing and having nice time. It was quite warm so I'd take my jacket off and put on the back of my chair with my bag. I not see anything suspicious, but when it time to pay, I put my jacket and felt for my wallet to get any money out, but the wallet gone. Someone must put their hand in my jacket pocket and taken it.

4 Circle the correct option in each phrase.

1 to send someone *in / to* prison

2 to plead guilty *of / to* a crime

3 to convict someone *of / for* a crime

4 to charge someone *of / with* a crime

5 to be tried *on / for* a crime

6 to be fined *with / for* doing something

5 Use the phrases in Exercise 4 to report what happened in each of these situations.

1 Policewoman: Mr Newman, you were caught taking goods from the electrical store. You will appear in court tomorrow.

The policewoman charged Mr Newman with shoplifting.

2 Judge: Mr Robbins, you will receive a prison sentence of two years for assault.

The judge _____

3 Lawyer: Did you take the car and drive it without the permission of the owner? And did you leave it by the side of the road close to where you live?

Jason: Yes, sir, I did.

Jason _____

4 Cheryl: Oh no, I've got a parking ticket. I've got to pay £60.

Graham: What for?

Cheryl: I parked on a double yellow line, but only for a couple of minutes.

Cheryl _____

5 Lawyer: Mr Johnson, you're on trial today for stealing a bike from outside the supermarket.

Mr Johnson _____

6 Judge: This court finds you are guilty of burglary, Mr Foster.

The court _____

Doing the right thing

1 **Read the descriptions of the situations and answer the questions.**

1 It was a very cold day. You were walking by a lake when you heard someone shouting 'Help!'. You saw a boy in the water who was in trouble. There was a sign which said 'Danger: deep water'. Next to the sign there was a life-saving ring on a rope and an emergency telephone. Above the phone were the words: 'Emergency Services: call 999'.

What would you have done first?

Then what would you have done?

What wouldn't you have done?

Give reasons for your answers.

First, I would have

_____

_____

_____

_____

_____

2 You were on your way to school when you noticed a group of three boys making fun of a younger boy. They'd taken his school bag and were throwing it to each other. The boy was clearly upset.

What would you have done first?

Then what would you have done?

What wouldn't you have done?

Give reasons for your answers.

_____

_____

_____

_____

_____

_____

_____

2 Match the two halves of each sentence. Then write complete sentences using the third conditional.

1 If the laptop (*not be*) on the table near the window,

2 If she (*not park*) her car on a double yellow line,

3 If you (*not leave*) the window open,

4 The judge (*not send*) him to prison

5 If we (*see*) his face more clearly,

6 I (*call*) the police straightaway

a if I (*notice*) the broken window as soon as I got home.

b the burglar (*not notice*) it.

c the thief (*not be able*) to get into the house.

d the traffic warden (*not give*) her a fine.

e we (*could / give*) you a better description of him.

f if he (*plead*) guilty.

1 _If the laptop hadn't been on the table near the window, the burglar wouldn't have noticed it._

2 _____

3 _____

4 _____

5 _____

6 _____

3 Rewrite these sentences using the third conditional.

1 He didn't put money into the parking meter so he got a fine.

If he had _put money into the parking meter, he wouldn't have got a fine._

2 I had my mobile phone with me so I was able to call the Emergency Services.

If I hadn't _____

3 I didn't know you were in trouble, so I didn't help you.

If I had _____

4 He robbed a bank so he went to prison.

If he hadn't _____

5 You looked out of the window so you saw the robbers escaping.

If you hadn't _____

The scene of the crime

1 This is a scene from a play called *The Davenport Diamond*. Look at it carefully.
What time of day is it? What time of year is it? _____

_____

2 One of the characters in the play is a detective. He interviews the only witness in the case, the
woman who saw what was happening in the library. In your notebook, write her answers.

Detective: Why did you go down to the library?

Witness: I couldn't sleep, so I went down to the library for a book. I heard a noise so I opened the
door slightly and then I saw him.

Detective: Who did you see and what was he doing?

Can you describe the man? What did he look like? What was he wearing?

What time was it and what else did you notice about the room? Doors, windows, lights,
that sort of thing?

3 This is the same scene from the play, but on a different night. Some of the details are different. What are they? Here is an example. Find ten more.

There isn't a lamp on the table but there is a candle burning.

1 _____

2 _____

3 _____

4 _____

5 _____

6 _____

7 _____

8 _____

9 _____

10 _____

All the world's a stage

1 Solve the crossword.

Across

3 A part played by an actor. (4)

5 A group of people chosen to decide the winner of a competition; a group of people chosen to decide if a person is guilty or not in a court of law. (4)

7 A person in a play or in a book. (9)

8 Something that covers all or part of your face. (4)

10 In Greek drama, a group of people who speak together, commenting on the action. (6)

14 Someone who writes plays. (10)

15 A play for the theatre; something unusual or exciting that happens. (5)

17 A play or film that makes you laugh. (6)

18 Lighting, sound and objects that are specially produced for the stage or a film, they make something that does not exist seem real. (7)

Down

1 To express your choice by officially writing a mark on a paper or by putting up your hand. (4)

2 Something you win in a competition. (5)

4 A large group of musicians who play together. (9)

6 Not real, created in the imagination. (9)

9 A serious play that ends sadly. (7)

10 Clothes worn by actors in a play. (8)

11 Based on facts and situations as they really are. (9)

12 A long poem, book or film which tells the story of people and events from the past. (4)

13 A small model of a person that you can move with strings or by putting your hand inside it. (6)

16 Greek and Roman amphitheatres had seats arranged in tiered _____. (4)

2 Match the words in the two columns and use them to complete the sentences.

open-	circle
semi-	air
horse-	known
make-	shoe
best-	up

Language tip

Remember that we use *used to* to talk about past habits.

Positive: *We used to go.*

Negative: *We didn't use to go.*

Questions: *Did you use to go?*

1   Actors on stage or in a film wear _____ to change their appearance or to emphasise certain features.

2   Make a _____ by folding a circle of paper in half. You can use this to make a basic theatrical mask.

3   The _____ shapes in the sand made the audience believe that a horse had passed by.

4   The Greeks and Romans performed their plays in _____ theatres.

5   William Shakespeare is the _____ English playwright.

3 Complete the conversation with *used to* and a verb from the box.

drop	have	not have	shout
go	have	open	sing

A: Oh, look! They've restored the old Astoria Cinema. I ¹_____ *used to go* _____ there every Saturday when I was your age. We ² _____ a TV at home, so going to the cinema was fantastic.

B: No TV? Really?

A: That's right. But we loved the cinema. It ³ _____ at 9 o'clock and we came out at mid-day.

B: So you were there all morning?

A: Yes. First we ⁴_____ a song. The words were projected onto a screen. Then there were cartoons like *Bugs Bunny* and *Tom and Jerry*. Next there was a news film. After that there were serials like *Flash Gordon* and *Superman*. And that was before the interval!

B: ⁵_____ popcorn?

A: No, we didn't. ⁶_____ an ice cream or an ice lolly. Sometimes the children sitting upstairs ⁷ _____ their lolly sticks on the children sitting below!

B: What happened after the interval?

A: That was when the main film came on. There were adventure films like *Tarzan* and there were westerns starring John Wayne. We ⁸ _____ and scream and cheer. It was very noisy but it was a lot of fun!

On stage, off stage

1 Complete the text with the words from the box.

actors	backstage crew	director	set designer
audience	costume designer	lighting and sound technicians	stage manager

People in the theatre

- It's the job of the ¹_____ to decide which plays are going to be put on and how they're going to be performed.
- The ²_____ bring characters to life on stage. They have to speak very clearly but they also use movement and expressions to communicate with the ³_____. They have to learn a lot of lines so of course they have to have a good memory.
- There's a ⁴_____, a very important person who is responsible for everything during a performance, including props and scene changes.
- The ⁵_____ decides what the stage will look like for each scene. He or she gives instructions to the scene painters and the scenery makers.
- The ⁶_____ has to find all the clothes that the actors wear.
- The ⁷_____ create some wonderful effects that add to what the actors are doing on stage. They have to be really skilled and good at interpreting the technical effects that the director wants.
- You don't see the ⁸_____ but they're just as important as all the others. They have to move heavy scenery quickly and efficiently and they sometimes have to build the sets.

Now, the stage set is a ship, just like this …

2 Choose the correct option. Then write the name of the job each sentence refers to.

1 You need to have a good memory to learn your (lines) / text. _____actor_____

2 You have to make sure the actors are *on scene / on stage* at the right time. _____

3 You need to be able to imagine what the *set / setting* will look like. _____

4 You need to know a lot about the history of fashion, particularly if the play is *put / set* in the past.
_____

5 You need to be able to use light to produce fantastic special *affects /effects*. _____

6 You need to have good woodworking skills because you may need to make *scenery / scenes*.
_____

3 In each pair of sentences, the underlined word in the first sentence gives a clue to the missing word in the second sentence. Write in the missing words.

1 She's a very well-known <u>director</u>. She's _____directed_____ a lot of plays.

2 Both of my parents are <u>actors</u>. I've always wanted to _____.

3 I like the <u>design</u> for the set. What's the name of the set _____?

4 He can <u>express</u> himself really well. He's got a great range of _____.

5 The director will make a <u>decision</u> about who to cast in the main role. She'll let you know when she's _____.

6 You have to be able to <u>speak</u> clearly and project your voice. Clear _____ and a strong voice are essential.

7 The director and the actors work on the <u>interpretation</u> of a play . There are different ways of _____ the same play.

8 This role is well within your <u>capability</u>. You are _____ of great things.

From script to performance

Writing Task

In *Diary of an (Un)teenager* do you remember how Spencer reacted when he found out that his friend, Zac, had become a skater?

> *Will I soon start throwing all my money away on stupid clothes?*
>
> *No, dear diary, I won't.*
>
> *I am going to stay EXACTLY as I am now.*
>
> *And that's a promise, signed here in my diary.*

What do you think happened next? In your notebook, write Scene 3 of the play.

Creative writing – getting started

Study tip

The most difficult part is starting. A lot of professional writers find it hard to fill the first page. The important thing is to write something. Remember you can change it afterwards.

Start with what you know. When writing Scene 3 of Zac's story, ask yourself, 'How would I feel if I were in Zac's position? What would I do? Who would I talk to?'

Title: **Scene:** Where does it take place? *At Spencer's house? At Zac's house? In town? At school?* **Characters:** Who is in the scene? *Spencer? Zac? Spencer's mum or dad? A school friend?* Give the stage directions in brackets. Include details of props and costumes. *What is Spencer wearing? What are the other characters wearing? Have the characters got anything with them, e.g. a mobile phone, a skateboard?* Write the characters' names in capital letters to show who is speaking. When a character starts to speak, put a colon (:) after their name. When a character comes on to the stage after the start of the scene, write 'Enter' followed by the name of the character. When they leave, write 'Exit' and the name of the character. Where necessary, describe how an actor should say the line.	**Diary** of an (Un)teenager **Scene 3:** _____ **Characters:** _____ _____ 

Well done!

You've now finished *Cambridge Global English Stage 9*. Take a moment to assess what you've done. Look back through your coursebook. Then in your notebook answer the questions.

Reading

Here are some examples of what you've read:

- a news article about twins being reunited
- a magazine article about the history of the polo shirt
- a timeline showing the history of recorded sound
- an extract from a book about the diet of a famous tennis player
- a newspaper article about the importance of getting a good night's sleep
- a feature about young entrepreneurs
- crime reports in newspapers
- poems and extracts from short stories, novels, a historical memoir, an autobiography.

What did you enjoy reading most and why?

Did you find any of the texts difficult? Which ones and why?

Writing

Here are some examples of what you have written:

- a paragraph about your family
- a note of apology to your teacher
- a summary of a story
- an article for a newspaper about banning mobile phones in school
- an end-of-term speech
- a profile of yourself as a learner
- a witness statement
- an application for a part-time job
- a script for a scene from a play.

Which piece of writing do you think was your best?

What do you find difficult about writing in English?

Listening

Here are some examples of what you've listened to:

- a conversation about careers
- interviews about what music means to people
- a news report about energy resources
- people giving opinions about fashion
- a telephone conversation about computer problems
- a presentation about jobs and careers
- a headteacher's speech
- a talk about jobs in the theatre.

What do you remember about the things you listened to?

Which do you find easier, listening or reading? Why?

Speaking

Here are some examples of what you've talked about:

- your family
- what music means to you
- diet and fitness
- attitudes to social media
- aspects of different jobs
- issues such as population changes
- naming traditions
- crime and punishment.

Do you feel confident when you're talking about these topics?

Do you need more practice in any of them?

Grammar reference

Grammar: Unit 1

both (of), each other / one another, either of / neither of

both

Use *both* to talk about two people (or things) together.

Both *my cousin and my best friend love surfing.*

My cousin and my best friend **both** *love surfing.*

Both comes <u>before</u> a main verb.

They **both** *love surfing.*

But it comes <u>after</u> the verb *to be* and auxiliary verbs.

They're **both** *good swimmers.*

They can **both** *swim really well.*

Both comes after a subject pronoun.

They **both** *love surfing.*

both of

Both of comes before object pronouns.

Both of *them love surfing.*

each other / one another

Each other and *one another* mean the same, but *each other* is used more often. You can use *one another* when you're making general statements.

My cousin and I talk to **each other** *every day.*

It's important to help **one another***.*

either of / neither of

Use *either of* when you mean 'one or the other'.

Has **either of** *your parents researched their family history?*

I've got two cousins in Canada but I've never met **either of** *them.*

Use *neither of* when you mean 'not one and not the other'.

Neither of *my cousins has been to see me.*

We usually use *either* and *neither* with a singular verb.

Reporting verbs

You can vary the way you report what someone said by using reporting verbs instead of *say* and *tell*.

verb + *to* infinitive

agree, decide, offer, promise, refuse, threaten

> *They decided to go to the sports centre.*
> *He promised to call us when he arrived.*

verb + object + *to* infinitive

advise, encourage, invite, remind, warn

> *Our teacher encouraged us to write a story for the competition.*
> *She reminded me to switch off my phone inside the theatre.*

verb + *-ing* form

deny, recommend, suggest

> *They recommended visiting the castle.*
> *She suggested going to the café in the museum.*

verb + preposition + *-ing* form

apologise, complain, insist

> *He apologised for arriving late.*
> *They insisted on taking us out for dinner.*

Verb + object + preposition + *-ing* form

accuse, blame, congratulate, forgive

> *My brother blamed me for breaking the window.*
> *She congratulated us on doing so well in our English exam.*

Grammar: Unit 2

-ing forms used as subjects, objects and after the verb *to be*

-ing forms used as subjects:
Listening to music helps me to relax.

-ing forms used as objects:
I really enjoy **swimming** in the sea.

-ing forms used after the verb *to be:*
The best thing about the start of term is **seeing** all your friends again.

Grammar: Unit 3

Degree and extreme adjectives

Use *very* with degree adjectives	Use *absolutely* with extreme adjectives
good	great / fantastic / marvellous / wonderful
bad	awful / terrible / horrible
big	enormous / huge
small	tiny / minute
happy	ecstatic / delighted
frightened / afraid	terrified
tired	exhausted
annoyed / angry	furious
surprised	amazed / astonished

Degree adjectives are also called 'scale' adjectives or 'gradable' adjectives.

extreme			extreme
(absolutely)	(very)	(very)	(absolutely)
great / fantastic	good	bad	awful / terrible

must have, might have, can't have + past participle

Use *must have* to talk about things you feel sure have happened.
Oh good. You're here already. You must have left home very early.

Use *might have* to talk about things which have perhaps happened.
I wonder why they're not here yet. There might have been a traffic jam on the motorway.

Use *can't have* to talk about things you feel sure haven't happened or about things that don't seem possible.
That pizza was enormous. You can't have eaten it already!

Remember to use the past participle after *must have, might have, can't have*. For irregular past participles, see pages 126 and 127.

Present continuous with *always*

You can use the present continuous with *always* to describe other people's annoying habits.
My little sister is always borrowing my clothes without asking. It really gets on my nerves.

You also use the present continuous with *always* when you're criticising yourself.
I'm always losing my keys.

Grammar: Unit 4

Question words as subjects and objects

who

Notice the difference in meaning between these two sentences:

1   *Who met you at the airport?*
2   *Who did you meet at the airport?*

In sentence 1, *who* is the subject of the question: 'When you arrived at the airport, who was there to meet you?'

In sentence 2, *who* is the object of the question: 'You met someone at the airport. Who was it?'

which

1   *Which came first, the book or the film?*
2   *Which did you like best, the book or the film?*

In sentence 1, *which* is the subject of the question.

In sentence 2, *which* is the object of the question.

what

1   *What happened to the main character in the book when he went into the old house?*
2   *What did the main character see when he went into the old house?*

In sentence 1, *what* is the subject of the question.

In sentence 2, *what* is the object of the question.

Grammar: Unit 5

Comparative adjectives

- For most one-syllable adjectives ending in -*e*, add -*r*   *close > closer*
- For other one-syllable adjectives, add -*er*   *long > longer*
- For two-syllable adjectives ending in -*y*, change the *y* to *i* and add -*er*   *easy > easier*
- For other two-syllable adjectives, use *more* in front of the adjective   *useful > more useful*
- For longer adjectives, use *more* in front of the adjective   *interesting > more interesting*

When an adjective ends in a single vowel and a single consonant, and the final syllable is stressed, double the consonant before adding -*er*.
big > bigger

To make negative comparisons use *less ... than.*
*I'm **less** shy now **than** I was when I was younger.*
*We go to the market because it's **less** expensive **than** the supermarket.*

Comparative adverbs

To make comparative adverbs add –*ly* to the adjective and use *more*.

easy > easily > more easily

To make negative comparisons, use *less* in front of the adverb.

less easily

Grammar: Unit 6

Pronouns expressing quantity in short answers

You can use these expressions as short answers without nouns, if the meaning is clear.

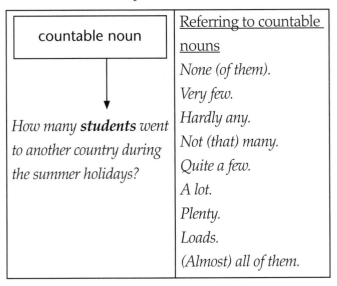

countable noun	Referring to countable nouns
*How many **students** went to another country during the summer holidays?*	*None (of them).* *Very few.* *Hardly any.* *Not (that) many.* *Quite a few.* *A lot.* *Plenty.* *Loads.* *(Almost) all of them.*

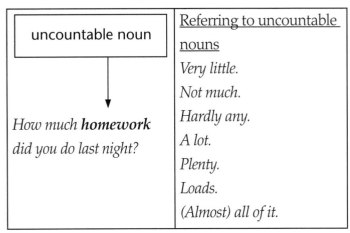

uncountable noun	Referring to uncountable nouns
*How much **homework** did you do last night?*	*Very little.* *Not much.* *Hardly any.* *A lot.* *Plenty.* *Loads.* *(Almost) all of it.*

Verbs followed by the *-ing* form

Remember that some verbs are followed by the *-ing* form.

admit	deny	give up	miss
avoid	dislike	hate	practise
can't help	don't mind	imagine	prefer
can't face	enjoy	involve	risk
can't stand	fancy	keep (on)	spend time
consider	feel like	like	suggest
delay	finish	love	waste time

Like, love, prefer and *hate* can be followed either by the *-ing* form or by the *to* infinitive.

Adverbs *just, really, still*

You can use *just, really* and *still* to add emphasis to what you're saying. They usually come before main verbs.
*I **just** wish I had more time.*
*I **still** get all my homework done.*
*I **really** enjoy listening to music.*

But notice that *just, still* and *really* usually come after the verb *to be*.
*I'm **just** fed up with listening to that song. Turn it off!*
*I'm **still** waiting for an answer.*
*It's **really** kind of you to offer to help.*

In negative sentences, *just, still* and *really* usually come before *not* if they emphasise the negative.
*I **just** don't have time.*
*I **still** haven't had time to watch the TV series I recorded.*
*I **really** don't have time to do all the things I'd like to do.*

Grammar: Unit 7

Determiners and pre-determiners

Determiners are words like *the, a / an, this, some, every*.

Pre-determiners are words that come before determiners to give more information or to give emphasis.

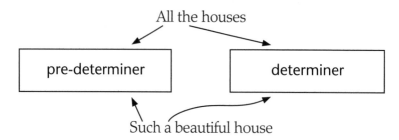

Note that you need to use *of* in the following expressions:

Every one of the *houses was different.*

Most of the *houses had a garden.*

Each of the *upstairs windows had a balcony.*

Which of these *houses do you like best?*

None of the *houses has been sold yet.*

Remember that *another* is written as one word, NOT ~~an other~~.

*The houses have **another** important feature: they are all carbon neutral.*

Future continuous

Use the future continuous to talk about what will be happening at a particular time in the future.

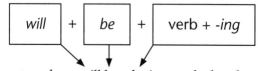

This time next week we will be relaxing on the beach.

	positive	negative	questions	short answers
Future continuous	I will be / I'll be relaxing on the beach.	I won't be sitting at home watching TV.	Will you be relaxing on the beach?	Yes, I will. / No, I won't.

You can also use the future continuous to refer to events that are due to happen or are likely to happen.

I'll be going *to the shops tomorrow. Do you want me to get you anything?*

Will you be going *to Australia again this year?*

Grammar: Unit 8

The passive

The passive is useful in phrases such as:

It is / was believed that

It is / was expected that

It is / was thought that

It is / was said that

It is / was suggested that

It means you don't have to specify exactly who believed, who expected, who thought, who said or who suggested something.

You can use an infinitive after a passive.

*You **are expected to complete** your project by the end of term.*

Past perfect continuous

Use the past perfect continuous to talk about actions or situations that had continued up to a time in the past.

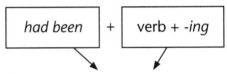

I'd been waiting for two hours outside the cinema when I realised I'd got the date wrong.

You can use the past perfect continuous to describe the cause of an action or a situation in the past.

I'd been eating chocolate so I wasn't at all hungry.

Relative pronouns

Remember to use *who* for people, *which / that* for things and *where* for places.

*The girl **who** lives at number 81 is my sister's best friend.*

*Selma, **who** lives at number 81, is my sister's best friend.*

*Did you enjoy the book **that / which** I lent you?*

*This book, **which** I've had since I was a child, belonged to my grandmother.*

*The house **where** my mum grew up is now a restaurant.*

*Hollywood, **where** lots of films are made, is in California.*

Grammar: Unit 9

Structures using comparatives and superlatives

You can use *more* and *(the) most, less* and *(the) least*

* before adjectives: *more / less / the least popular*
* before nouns: *more / less / the least interest* (but use *few* and *the fewest* with plural nouns: *fewer spectators / the fewest spectators*)
* before adverbs: *more / less / the least quickly*

The following words are both adjectives and adverbs: *fast, long, high, early, late, hard, near, soon.*

For both adjectives and adverbs, add *-(e)r* to make the comparative and *-(e)st* to make the superlative: *faster, fastest.*

Note that you say *less fast, the least fast.*

_____

Answer to the pizza puzzle on page 57.

Grammar: Unit 10

Prepositional and phrasal verbs

Prepositional verbs are verbs which are closely linked with certain prepositions. For example: *rely on, depend on.*

Phrasal verbs are verbs which are followed by a preposition or an adverbial particle. For example:
Put *your books* **on** *my desk* (verb + preposition*)*
Put *your jacket* **on** (verb + adverbial particle)

You don't need to understand the differences to be able to use these verbs. Just learn them as complete phrases.

Reported speech – statements

Remember that when we tell people what someone said, we usually change the tense because what they said was in the past.

am / are / is	→	was / were
have / has	→	had
can	→	could
will	→	would
do / does	→	did
present simple	→	past simple
past simple	→	past perfect
present perfect	→	past perfect

Grammar: Unit 11

Prepositional and phrasal verbs to do with learning

keep up with

catch up on

come up with (an answer)

do without something

fall behind

finish off (a piece of work)

get away with

go over (something)

hand in (your homework)

join in

look up

make up (an answer)

put (something) across

put off (doing something)

read through (run through / go through)

run out (of time)

work out

Prepositional and phrasal verbs have two or even three parts.

*I'm not very good at **looking up** words in a dictionary.*

*I try to **get away with** doing as little as possible.*

You can say:

*I'm not very good at **looking up** words in a dictionary.*

OR

*I'm not very good at **looking** words **up** in a dictionary.*

But if the object is a pronoun (for example, *them* rather than *words*), you must separate the two parts of the verb.

*I'm not very good at **looking them up** in a dictionary.*

NOT

~~I'm not very good at looking up them in a dictionary.~~

Quantifiers with uncountable nouns

Advice and *equipment* are uncountable nouns. You can't talk about ~~an advice / some advices, an equipment / some equipments~~.

But you can talk about *a piece of advice* and *items of equipment*.

I have to give you just one piece of advice.

There are various items of equipment you need.

Present perfect simple and present perfect continuous

We use the present perfect **simple** to talk about past actions that are relevant now.

*We've **had** permission from the headteacher to organise a school trip.*

We use the present perfect **continuous** to talk about actions which started in the past and are still going on.

*We've **been learning** about weather patterns and climate this term.*

We also use the present perfect continuous for actions that have just happened and have visible results.

A: *Your hands are covered in oil.*

B: *Yes, I've **been repairing** my bike.*

Grammar: Unit 12

Reflexive pronoun structures

Subject pronoun	Reflexive pronoun
I	myself
you	yourself
he, she, it	himself, herself, itself
we	ourselves
you	yourselves
they	themselves

Use reflexive pronouns with verbs when the object is the same person (or thing) as the subject.

*I made **myself** a toasted cheese sandwich.*

*If you set the timer, the oven will turn **itself** off when the food is ready.*

Do not use reflexive pronouns with these verbs:

get up, wash, feel, relax, hurry.

Notice the difference between:

*They looked at **themselves**. (They looked at their own reflection in a mirror.)*

AND

They looked at each other. (Each person looked at the other person.)

Notice also:

They have known each other for a long time.

NOT

~~They have known themselves for a long time.~~

You can use reflexive pronouns for emphasis:

*I made these biscuits **myself**.*

Present continuous passive

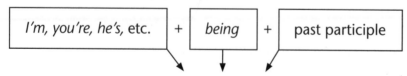

*This term **we're being taught** French by a French native speaker.*

*The swimming pool **isn't being used** at the moment.*

*Are the auditions **being held** in the main hall?*

Grammar: Unit 13

Prepositions in the context of numbers and data

Notice the prepositions used <u>before</u> these noun phrases:

in each age group
under the age of 5
between the ages of 0 and 30
about 50%
from 100 *to* 150
over half

Notice the prepositions used <u>after</u> these noun phrases and verbs:

an increase / a rise *in*
a decline / a fall *in*
(it) fell *to*
(it) rose *to*
(it) increased *to*

The future perfect

We use the future perfect to say that something will have happened by a certain time in the future.

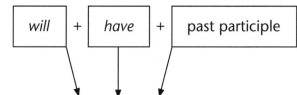

By 2050…

the temperature on earth **will have risen** due to global warming.
the world's population **won't have decreased**.

Conjunctions

Conjunctions join phrases and clauses in a sentence.

Joining phrases

either ... or
neither ... nor
both ... and ...

We can **either** cycle into town **or** take the bus.
We can meet **either** at my house **or** in town.
Neither my sister **nor** I like coffee.
Both my brother **and** I play badminton.

Joining clauses

after	so
although	so that
as	until
before	when
provided (that)	whereas
since	while

Although I was tired, I stayed up to watch the film.
After I'd seen the film, I couldn't sleep!
As I didn't have any homework, I played football after school.
It was hot **so** we spent the morning at the swimming pool.

Grammar: Unit 14

Participle clauses

Past participle clauses are used more often in written English than in spoken English.

Discovered by Alexander Fleming, penicillin became the first antibiotic.
Letters posted after 5 o'clock will not be delivered the following day.

Present participles can also be used in participle clauses.
I saw a policeman running down the street. (= I saw a policeman who was running down the street.)

You can use present participles instead of a conjunction to combine ideas.
We were at the café waiting for you. (= We were at the café and we were waiting for you.)
Realising that my mobile phone was still on, I quickly turned it off. (= When I realised that my mobile was still on, I quickly turned it off.)
I hurt my ankle playing football. (= I hurt my ankle while I was playing football.)
Feeling bored, I decided to see if my friend wanted to go out. (= I decided to see if my friend wanted to go out because I was feeling bored.)

Present participles can also be used after the conjunctions *before* and *after*.
Before going to bed, make sure you brush your teeth.
After hearing the song on the radio, I downloaded it.

Present simple passive

We often use the passive when describing formal occasions because it is the actions that are important, not who does them.

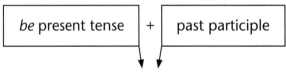

$$\boxed{be \text{ present tense}} + \boxed{\text{past participle}}$$

A garden party is held every year in July.

Filming is not permitted during the performance.
Are children invited to the ceremony?

Grammar: Unit 15

Prepositional and phrasal verbs to do with using technology

switch on	attach to	zoom in (on)	click on
switch off	hold down	log in	fill in
back up	scroll down	type in	print out

Focusing adverbs

Focusing adverbs focus your attention on a thing or an action. They include:

especially	only
generally	just
mainly	particularly
even	simply

I **only** went out for five minutes.

It's **just** a short walk to the park.

I **simply** don't understand.

The concert was **particularly** good.

Adverbs of degree

Adverbs of degree modify adjectives or other adverbs. Examples include:

a bit	rather
a lot	slightly
absolutely	too
extremely	totally
quite	very

It's very easy to make mistakes when you're in a hurry.

It's a lot harder to play well when you're nervous.

The documentary was extremely interesting.

The plot of the soap opera was totally ridiculous.

I'm slightly anxious about travelling on my own.

Extremely and totally are like very but they're stronger.

Quite can mean 'a bit' or it can mean 'very', depending on how you say it and how you say the word that follows it.

It's quite <u>nice</u>. (= It's good.)

It's <u>quite</u> nice. (= It's OK but it isn't great.)

Rather is stronger than quite.

Grammar: Unit 16

Prepositional phrases

Certain prepositions are commonly combined with certain nouns.

at the cinema / at the theatre

at university

at an angle

a play by Shakespeare

a painting by Leonardo da Vinci

on TV

on the radio

on the surface

on page 29

in a picture / a photo

in a certain way

in Moscow

Conjunctions followed by *-ing* forms

Some conjunctions are followed by *-ing* forms.

after

before

when

while

since

Be careful when crossing the road.

I can work well while listening to music.

Since taking up judo, she's become much more confident.

Grammar: Unit 17

Prepositional verbs to do with crime

to charge (someone) with (a crime)

to plead guilty to (a crime)

to convict someone of (a crime)

to send someone to prison

to be tried for (a crime)

to fine someone for (doing something wrong)

The third conditional

We use the third conditional to talk about imagined situations in the past – things that did not happen.

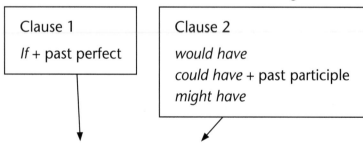

Clause 1	Clause 2
If + past perfect	*would have* *could have* + past participle *might have*

If you had asked me, I would have helped you.

You can reverse the order of the clauses:

I would have helped you if you had asked me.

Grammar: Unit 18

Used to and *would*

You can use *used to* and *would* to refer to past habits.

When I was a child, I used to play outside every evening.

When I was a child, I would play outside every evening.

	positive	negative	questions	short answers
used to	I used to play outside every evening.	I didn't use(d) to spend much time inside.	Did you use(d) to play outside every evening?	Yes, I did. / No, I didn't.

But notice that <u>only</u> *used to* can be used for past states, e.g. with verbs *be, have, live.*

I used to have short hair. NOT ~~I would have short hair.~~

Prepositions following nouns and adjectives

It's important to know which prepositions follow certain nouns and adjectives. Here are some examples:

nouns

congratulations on

difficulty with

reason for

responsibility for

adjectives

anxious about

knowledgeable about

worried about

clever at

good at

shocked at / by

surprised at / by

responsible for

sorry for

different from

afraid / frightened of

capable of

dressed in

interested in

nice to

good with

disappointed with

wrong with

pleased with

Irregular verbs

Some past tenses are irregular, and so are some past participles.

Infinitive	Past simple	Past participle
be	was / were	been
beat	beat	beaten
become	became	become
begin	began	begun
bend	bent	bent
bite	bit	bitten
blow	blew	blown
break	broke	broken
bring	brought	brought
build	built	built
burst	burst	burst
buy	bought	bought
catch	caught	caught
choose	chose	chosen
come	came	come
cost	cost	cost
cut	cut	cut
do	did	done
draw	drew	drawn
drink	drank	drunk
drive	drove	driven
eat	ate	eaten
fall	fell	fallen
feed	fed	fed
feel	felt	felt
fight	fought	fought

Infinitive	Past simple	Past participle
find	found	found
fly	flew	flown
forbid	forbade	forbidden
forget	forgot	forgotten
forgive	forgave	forgiven
freeze	froze	frozen
get	got	got
give	gave	given
go	went	gone / been
grow	grew	grown
hang	hung	hung
have	had	had
hear	heard	heard
hide	hid	hidden
hit	hit	hit
hold	held	held
hurt	hurt	hurt
keep	kept	kept
kneel	knelt	knelt
know	knew	known
lay	laid	laid
lead	led	led
leave	left	left
lend	lent	lent
let	let	let
lie	lay	lain

Infinitive	Past simple	Past participle
light	lit	lit
lose	lost	lost
make	made	made
mean	meant	meant
meet	met	met
pay	paid	paid
put	put	put
read	read	read
ride	rode	ridden
ring	rang	rung
rise	rose	risen
run	ran	run
say	said	said
see	saw	seen
sell	sold	sold
send	sent	sent
set	set	set
sew	sewed	sewn / sewed
shake	shook	shaken
shine	shone	shone
shoot	shot	shot
show	showed	shown
shrink	shrank	shrunk
shut	shut	shut
sing	sang	sung
sink	sank	sunk

Infinitive	Past simple	Past participle
sit	sat	sat
sleep	slept	slept
slide	slid	slid
speak	spoke	spoken
spend	spent	spent
split	split	split
spread	spread	spread
stand	stood	stood
steal	stole	stolen
stick	stuck	stuck
sting	stung	stung
sweep	swept	swept
swim	swam	swum
swing	swung	swung
take	took	taken
teach	taught	taught
tear	tore	torn
tell	told	told
think	thought	thought
throw	threw	thrown
understand	understood	understood
wake (up)	woke (up)	woken (up)
wear	wore	worn
weep	wept	wept
win	won	won
write	wrote	written

Acknowledgements

The authors and publishers acknowledge the following sources of copyright material and are grateful for the permissions granted. While every effort has been made, it has not always been possible to identify the sources of all the material used, or to trace all copyright holders. If any omissions are brought to our notice, we will be happy to include the appropriate acknowledgements on reprinting.

Unit 2 history of football kits text copyright © Historical Football Kits; Unit 4 excerpt from The People's Century by Godfrey Hodgson, published by BBC Books, reprinted by permission of The Random House Group Limited; Unit 8 excerpt from Berzok, Linda Murray 'Potato' Encyclopedia of Food and Culture, 1E © 2003 Gale, a part of Cengage Learning, Inc., reproduced by permission www.cengage.com/permissions; Unit 11 KidZania London: Children are in charge in real life toy town by Lizzie Edmonds, published June 2015, copyright © The Evening Standard; Unit 14 excerpt from The Cambridge Encyclopedia of the English Language by David Crystal, 1995, 2003, published by Cambridge University Press

Thanks to the following for permission to include images:

Cover mtphoto19/Alamy Stock Photo; p.5 *top row* kurhan/Shutterstock; p.5 *middle row l to r* iko/Shutterstock, vgstudio/Shutterstock, stockyimages/Shutterstock, Cristian Zamfir/Shutterstock, vgstudio/Shutterstock, Valua Vitaly/Shutterstock; p.5 *bottom row l* Tompet/Shutterstock, *r* Ewais/Shutterstock; p.6 Lars Baron/Getty Images; p.7 Monkey Business Images/Shutterstock; p.10*t* ffolas/Shutterstock; p.10*m* Mikhail Khusid/Shutterstock; p.10*b* windu/Shutterstock; p.11*l* DESHAKALYAN CHOWDHURY/Stringer/Getty Images; p.11*r* Josef Polleross/Getty Images; p.14 Popperfoto/Getty Images; p.15 Mitch Gunn/Shutterstock; p.20 iQoncept/Shutterstock; p.23 peresanz/Shutterstock; p24. Milkovasa/Shutterstock, DK Arts/Shutterstock, Maximus256/Shutterstock, marijaf/Shutterstock, furtseff/Shutterstock, pbombaert/Shutterstock, Andrey_Popov/Shutterstock, Skylines/Shutterstock, Matthias G. Ziegler/Shutterstock, ayzek/Shutterstock, Chromakey/Shutterstock, 3DMAVR/Shutterstock, Florin Burlan/Shutterstock; p.29 Zern Liew/Shutterstock; p.32 Portrait of a Lady thought to be Lady Mary Wortley Montagu (1689-1762) (oil on panel), Knapton, George (1698-1778)/Private Collection/Photo © Christie's Images/Bridgeman Images; p.44 Christos Georghiou/Shutterstock; p.48 Mary Evans Picture Library; p.50*l* Evgeniya Pushai/Shutterstock, *m* Anna Rassadnikova/Shutterstock, *r* Popmarleo/Shutterstock; p.51 Bettman/Getty Images; p.52 Shelby Allison/Shutterstock; p.54 Monkey Business Images/Shutterstock; p.69 Tim P. Whitby/Stringer/Getty Images; p.73 Matthew Cole/Shutterstock; p.88*l* chrisdorney/Shutterstock, *m* Tamas Panczel – Eross/Shutterstock, *r* hfng/Shutterstock; p.90 © THE UNSEEN 2016; p.91 Brian B. Bettencourt/Getty Images; p.93 © 2015 Sensing Umbrella; p.102 computerman/Shutterstock; p.110 prudkov/Shutterstock

Illustrations © Cambridge University Press: p.12 Phillip Burrows; pp.17, 19, 75, 95, 99, 108 David Banks; pp.35, 53, 57, 78, 79,118 Sharpe Images; pp.40, 42, 81 Mark Turner/Beehive Illustration; pp.67, 98, 104, 105 Dylan Gibson; p.72 Belinda Evans